Grace Under Fire

Grace Under Fire

Letters of Faith in Times of War

EDITED BY

Andrew Carroll

DOUBLEDAY

New York London Toronto
Sydney Auckland

PUBLISHED BY DOUBLEDAY

Copyright © 2007 by Andrew Carroll

All Rights Reserved

Published in the United States by Doubleday, an imprint of The Doubleday Broadway
Publishing Group, a division of Random House, Inc., New York.
www.doubleday.com

DOUBLEDAY and the portrayal of an anchor with a dolphin are registered
trademarks of Random House, Inc.

Book design by rlf design

Library of Congress Cataloging-in-Publication Data
    Grace under fire : letters of faith in times of war / edited by Andrew Carroll—1st ed.
        p.   cm.
        1. United States—History, Military—Sources.   2. United States—Religious life and
    customs—Sources.   3. Soldiers—United States—Correspondence.   4. Soldiers—
    Religious life—United States—History—Sources.   5. War—Religious aspects—History—
    Sources.   6. United States—Armed Forces—Biography.   7. Soldiers' writings,
    American.   8. American letters.   I. Carroll, Andrew.
        E181.G73   2007
        355.00973—dc22   2006034027

ISBN 978-0-385-51974-8

PRINTED IN THE UNITED STATES OF AMERICA

10 9 8 7 6 5 4 3 2 1

First Edition

*To our nation's military chaplains
and the other brave souls who have brought—
and continue to bring—words of faith
to American troops around the world.*

They can laugh about foxhole religion but every front line soldier embraces a little religion and are not ashamed to pray. When you face death hourly and daily you can't help but believe in Divine Guidance. My faith in God has increased a thousand fold. He pulled me thru when nothing else could. . . .

The weather is still terrible rain & snow flurries all the time, my feet haven't been dry for over a week. I'm trying to write as I duck down in my hole every time I hear artillery shells whistle towards me. They are bursting all around and I wonder when one will have my name on it. We were pulled out for a couple of hours to see a show the other day. I saw Marlene Dietrich and her show in person a few miles back. They held it in a shell splattered Catholic Church. It's really a pity these beautiful old churches being devastated over here.

Well dear I guess I better get down and stay down. I don't like these "incoming mail deliveries" and seen too many hit by not being down. So all my love dear. Your hubby, Al

—Thirty-two-year-old Sergeant Alvin McAnney Jr.,
writing to his wife in the fall of 1944 in Luxembourg

Opposite:
A lone American soldier stands inside a bombed-out
church "somewhere in Europe."

◦⇌ Grace Under Fire ⇌◦

The scorched and water-damaged prayer book that survived the fire that destroyed the Carroll family's home

confession: Years ago, after I started seeking out and preserving wartime letters, I came to the conclusion that God did not exist.

I hadn't always been a nonbeliever. I was raised in a conservative, Christian household, and although I had questioned my faith as a teenager, by the time I graduated in 1988, I felt that I had truly embraced Christianity with all my heart and soul.

And then two weeks before Christmas 1989, when I was a sophomore in college, my father called from Washington, D.C., with terrible news—a fire had swept through our home and destroyed almost everything we owned. He was phoning from a neighbor's house while watching firefighters douse the few stubborn, remaining flames as we spoke.

I had just started preparing for my midterm exams and was looking forward to coming home to celebrate the holidays. "Home" was now gone. We moved into a rental property several blocks away as our house, burned beyond recognition, was rebuilt.

Initially, I was so grateful that my father wasn't caught up in the blaze and had escaped unharmed that my faith in God was actually strengthened by the experience. (Even our little beige cat, Claude, had bounded out safely, though he did seem a bit perplexed by the whole incident, wondering what on earth we had done to *his* house.) One of the only possessions of mine to survive was my grandmother's prayer book. Slightly charred and water damaged, it was in relatively good condition; a small miracle among the ashes.

For me, the worst thing about the fire was losing all of my letters. They weren't Civil War missives or correspondence from any conflict, just personal letters from old friends traveling overseas, high school classmates describing their first year in college, and my parents, who had written me poignant messages at significant moments in my life. While not historically significant, the letters were a tangible connection to loved ones and a priceless record of cherished memories. And then, on that day in mid-December, they literally went up in smoke.

Over the next few years I became more interested in handwritten correspondence, especially as e-mail became more prevalent, and I was curious to know what other people did with their old letters. I was shocked to find that many veterans I talked to said that they had tossed their wartime letters in the garbage. Some felt that their children wouldn't want them, and they were all very modest about their time in the military. "I was no hero," one former soldier insisted. "I wasn't a general or anyone famous, just a young grunt doing my job." No one in my immediate family had ever served in the armed forces, and I grew up not knowing a single person in uniform. Nevertheless, it seemed to me that, when veterans threw away their old letters, we were losing something as a nation.

In the summer of 1998, I decided to start an informal effort called the Legacy Project to encourage Americans to save their wartime correspondence. On a whim, I wrote to "Dear Abby" and asked if she could promote the initiative to her readers. Much to my surprise, "Dear Abby" said yes. I was thrilled but, as it turned out, totally unprepared emotionally and logistically for what was going to happen next.

Three days after the "Dear Abby" column ran on November 11, 1998, a clerk from my neighborhood post office, where I had set up a small PO box, called and asked, "Is this Andrew Carroll?" He did not sound pleased.

"Yes," I responded hesitantly.

"You need to come down here *now* and get your mail."

I apologized profusely and said I would bike over immediately.

"Bring a car," the clerk advised.

Sure enough, I had bins and bins of mail waiting to be picked up. I vividly remember sitting outside the post office in my car, tearing open the envelopes and discovering letters from every major U.S. conflict: the American Revolution, the Civil War, World Wars I and II, Korea, Vietnam, Desert Storm, and even peace-keeping efforts in the Balkans. (The wars in Iraq and Afghanistan were still years away.)

What I was not expecting were the personal messages to me from the spouses, parents, and siblings of the veterans who had written the enclosed war letters. Mothers shared with me stories about their young sons, some of them only teenage boys, whose lives were cut short in Vietnam. The adult children of men killed in Korea or World War II explained to me what it was like growing up without a dad and how they got to know him only through the letters he had written home before dying. And the wives of combat veterans described how their husbands had returned to the States completely changed and had refused to talk about the terrible things they had seen firsthand.

The war letters themselves chronicled these horrible sights in unflinching detail: innocent civilians caught in the crossfire during major battles, the wholesale destruction of entire towns and cities, close buddies getting killed or grotesquely wounded, and, in some of the World War II letters, the mass graves and concentration camps that held the bodies of countless men, women, and children murdered by the Nazis.

Certainly I was aware of the harsh brutality of war before I launched the Legacy Project, but in going through letter after letter, it was no longer remote and abstract. It had become shockingly real and human. I was reading the names of the people impacted by this violence, seeing the images they were recording, and hearing the anguish in their voices. The endless accounts of terror and cruelty became unbearable, and one question began to consume me: "Why does God allow such evil to continue?" My heart had become so hardened that I no longer even tried to listen for an answer. My mind was made up. God, I decided, must not exist.

But while I had given up on God, He had not given up on me. I discovered, like most who have lost faith at some point in their lives, that He never stops sending us messages of hope. Sometimes we're just unable or unwilling to see them.

As I kept reading the letters pouring in from all around the country, I started to find letters by troops who had reflected on the very same doubts I was raising. "How can there be fairness in one man being maimed for life, suffering agonies, another killed instantaneously, while I get out of it safe?" a young private fighting in World War I named Walter Bromwich wrote to his pastor back in Pennsylvania. "Does God really love us individually or does He love His purpose more?" Bromwich, however, had maintained his faith. "What I would like to believe is that God is in this war, not as a spectator, but backing up everything that is good in us," he went on. "I don't know whether God goes forth with armies but I do know that He is in lots of our men or they would not do what they do."

Almost ninety years later a U.S. Army officer and doctor, Scott Barnes, who was treating the wounded in Iraq, sent his friends and family an e-mail that also tried to answer the question, Where is God? "He is in the O[perating] R[oom] guiding the hands of the surgeons," Barnes wrote. "He is in the will of the sergeants helping organize a blood drive as only they can, He is in the hearts of the soldiers who immediately rolled up their sleeves to give what they had to save a dying brother whom they don't even know."

One by one, letters like these began to reveal themselves, and I was struck by their diversity. Fathers deploying overseas wrote touching letters to their children, encouraging them to "take care of mommy" and dedicate their lives to God. Troops who had survived hellish battles and, in one case, the sinking of a ship, described how they had put their trust in God and made it through unscathed. Sweethearts exchanged heartfelt messages promising to stay true to each other no matter what temptations were laid out before them during their separation. Military chaplains put themselves in harm's way to offer words of comfort to frontline troops in need of spiritual guidance. Family members on the home front, who represent the unacknowledged heroes of every conflict, repeatedly reminded their loved ones fighting abroad how proud they were of them as they waited anxiously for their return. Overall, the letters I was finding were riveting, poetic, candid, and intimate, and they accentuated the bravery and decency of those who serve. And, most of all, they spoke profoundly not only of destruction and death, but of everlasting life.

The Marines, soldiers, airmen, and sailors who wrote these letters were hardly naïve about the realities of battle; indeed, most were seasoned combat veterans who had seen the worst of human nature and still held fast to their beliefs. "Perhaps some may feel that we are in vain and view the eventualities of war through rose-colored glasses, but if that were so, then how could we believe in prayer and that a world of peace is possible?" a Jewish soldier named Joseph Portnoy wrote to his wife, Ruth, in August 1944. "No," he went on, "as long as we can believe that our lives are still molded by God's will, and believe in his justice, we can never be accused of deliberately sugarcoating our senses."

The faith of these young men and women, who were insightful beyond their years, had a profound impact on me. The beauty and wisdom of their words and the courage of their actions both inspired and humbled me. Most important, they revived my faith in God. They made me a believer again and showed me, as I hope they will show others, that even in the bleakest of circumstances, with God's help, we can overcome all adversity. Through Him, we can endure any hardship. Because of Him, we are never alone.

At its heart, this book is not about war. It is about courage, devotion, honor, resilience, and, of course, faith. It is about individuals who have encountered trials that rival the burdens of Job and have nevertheless persevered. Even if we are not in the military, every one of us wages smaller, more personal battles each day—against despair, sin, and doubt—and these letters are a powerful reminder that no matter how tough the contest, there is always reason for hope.

Ultimately, the extraordinary individuals featured in this book have not just written about genuine faith, they have lived it. They have risked their lives for others, demonstrated compassion to those in need, and, despite all that has been demanded of and sometimes even taken from them, expressed only gratitude for the blessings they do have. They embody the words found in 1 Peter (5:10): "The God of all grace," the scripture reads, "after you have suffered a little while, will himself restore you and make you strong, firm and steadfast." And they have shown to me—as I hope they will to others—the true meaning of faith and that there is no greater victory than to have one's belief in God restored.

With trust in Him, life's battles are already won.

The American Revolution

James Williams, Serving in the War of Independence, Tells His Son Daniel That He Is Off Fighting in Defense of Their "Rights and Liberties"

Few letters by U.S. troops who fought in the American Revolution exist today. Compared to other major conflicts in our nation's history, not as many letters were written; there was no postal system to speak of, paper was scarce, and a significant number of soldiers were illiterate. Unfortunately, of the letters that were sent from the front lines (and they were usually hand-delivered through an informal network), many were lost or damaged over time. But what is remarkable about the relatively small number of letters that have survived is how similar the sentiments are to those expressed in correspondence written today. The language is much more formal, but the emotions are very much the same. On June 12, 1779, thirty-eight-year-old James Williams of Hanover, Virginia, penned the following letter to his son Daniel, explaining to him that he is now the man of the house and to place his trust in God.

Dear Son:

This is the first chance I have had to write you. I am, by the cause of Providence, in the field in defence of my country. When I reflect on the matter, I feel myself distracted on both hands by this thought, that in my old age I should be obliged to take the field in defence of my rights and liberties, and that of my children. God only knows that it is not of choice, but of necessity, and from the consideration that I had rather suffer anything than lose my birthright, and that of my children.

When I come to lay down in the field, <u>stripped</u> of all the pleasure that my family connections afford me at home—surrounded by an affectionate wife and eight dear children, and all the blessings of life—when I reflect on my own distress, I feel for that of my family, on account of my absence from their midst; and especially for the mother, who sits like a dove that has lost its mate, having the weight of the family on her shoulders.

These thoughts make me afraid that the son we so carefully nursed in our youth may do something that would grieve his mother. Now, my son, if my favor is worth seeking, let me tell you the only step to procure it is the care of your tender mother—to please her is ten times more valuable than any other favor that you could do me in my person.

I am sorry to have to inform you of the melancholy death of Anthony Griffin, which took place on the 11th instant, while out with a scouting party. Alighting from his horse, and leaning on his gun, it accidentally went off, shooting him through the head. He never spoke after the accident. This is a fatal consequence of handling guns without proper care; they ought to be used with the greatest caution. The uncertainty of life ought to induce every man to prepare for death.

Now, my son, I must bid you farewell. I commit you to the care of Providence, begging that you will try to obtain that peculiar blessing. May God bless you, my son, and give you grace to conduct yourself, in my absence, as becomes a dutiful son to a tender mother and the family.

I am in reasonable good health at present, and the regiment as much so as could be expected. The death of Griffin is much lamented. I hope in God this will find you, my son, and your dear mother and the children, all well. My best compliments to you all, and all enquiring friends.

I am, dear son, with great respect, your affectionate father,
Jas. Williams

Before Facing His Brother Percival in Battle During the Civil War, Thomas Drayton Castigates Him for Turning Against His Native Land—and God

&

Percival Drayton Writes to a Cousin About the South's "Unholy Rebellion"

As the War of Independence represented a conflict between a young country and its motherland, the Civil War was figuratively—and, at times, literally—a clash between brothers. Thomas Fenwick Drayton and his younger brother Percival were originally from South Carolina, but their father, a congressman named William Drayton, moved the family to Pennsylvania after he retired from public office. The brothers had relatives and acquaintances in both the North and South, and, as tensions between the two regions escalated, Percival believed that his loyalty should be to their adopted home and, more important, the United States of America. Both men, it turned out, believed they were on the side of God. On May 1, 1861, Thomas wrote his brother the following letter.

My dear Percy

I returned last night from Montgomery—where I had been on some postal matters, in anticipation of the period when the Contracts at Washington, shall have been annulled by those who hold hateful dominion there. And how you Percival

9

Drayton can consent to hold a commission under a Government—whom I know you cannot sympathise with—and whose vandal atrocity in the imitation of a most cruel war, clearly indicate what more atrocious & bloodthirsty attempts at <u>subjugation</u> will hereafter be attempted, such as stealing negroes, burning houses, John Brown raids to butcher helpless women & children, cut the dikes of the Mississippi and drown thousands of families "like rats in the hold of a ship." These & Such incursions & barbarities with which we are threatened by the northern borders—who already possess the reins of Government—if that can be called one,—where universal terror reigns as freedom of opinion is denied.

But enough—it wont do for you and I to quarrel—though in politics, we are divided. I had understood at our last interview—that although you would not take sides with the South—you would not do what you now have done,—take position against her, but that, you would resign and return to private life! But this is impossible—you cannot at such a crisis be a <u>neutral</u>. William Drayton—had he not died—would never have acted with you and retained a commission under an administration whose acts show it lost to all sense of justice, magnanimity and honesty, and in this hour of heartfelt sorrow, I pray Almighty God, that your convictions of duty—will never prompt you to set foot upon your native land as one of Lincoln's brutal cohorts, breathing fire & destruction upon a people who to repeated overtures of peace and earnest demands to pursue their own destiny in their own way, have been replied to with taunts and the sword brandished over their heads with the scornful division of presumptuous superiority, as from a superior race.

But henceforth, Percival Drayton, believe the South like yourselves a <u>unit</u>—and thus we shall enter upon this conflict <u>forced</u> upon us—in our faith—and relying upon God to maintain the justness of our causes, fighting manfully for our houses & rights;—and understand my brother that when the olive branch of peace is next offered, it will be extended by other hands than ours.—

Farewell Percy—and however much we may differ on the present issue—let no unkind word escape—to lacerate the heart of the other. Defend the soil of Pennsylvania if you will. Then, you and I will never meet as armed foes;—cross her Southern boundary—with hostile purpose—and we shall face each other—as brothers never should.

Love to my poor, dear old Mother—may God bless & sustain her at this terrible moment.—

Your affect brother
Thos F Drayton

Percival's response to this letter has been lost, but Thomas alludes to it in what would be his last message to his brother for the duration of the war. "I have just rec^d yours of the 6th inst," Thomas wrote on May 10, "and cannot but lament that our political views are so widely different, and that your arguments should afford so convincing a proof that prejudice had evidently usurped the seat of sound judgment." Thomas then bid his brother adieu: "I will keep this remarkable epistolary effusion of yours— for I am sure in less than a year, you will candidly disavow the assertions & opinions therein expressed." In less than a year, in fact, they would be exchanging not words, but gunfire; Thomas and Percival Drayton were the only two brothers in the war to command opposing forces in the same battle (Port Royal, November 1861). Percival would prevail, but in a letter written to a cousin, Heyward Drayton, on January 10, 1862, he was not in the mood to boast of the Union victory. Instead, he was saddened that members of their family—like the country itself—were at arms against each other, especially at a time when his mother was gravely ill. Percival, who was the captain of the USS Pochahontas, also wanted to address a question his cousin had raised about whether or not he was illegally protecting runaway slaves on his ship. "My dear Heyward," Percival wrote,

As you well say it is possible to go through the forms of Merry Christmas and happy new year but not these times at least to us they have no substance, as peculiarly to us this war has subverted the best formations of happiness and family union. And in addition death seems to be looming in the distance over those who are dear to us. . . . I hope that I may see my mother again although I am afraid it is without reason that I do so. She will at least when God shall call her away be always in my memory as the embodyment of unselfish love and Christian charity. . . .

As regard to this war its end looks to me everyday further and further off, and indeed with the evident desperation of the Southern people, and our luke-warmness, I can see nothing to terminate it. . . . If you will look at the report of the Secretary of the Navy, you will find that we are directed to take charge of and protect refugees from the insurgent districts without regard to colour, and this is all I have ever done. The fact is that when the poor creatures come into me, fright-ened to death from having been hunted down and shot at, and I know if I sent them away it will be merely to expose them to a continuation of the same treat-ment, I cannot enter cooly into a discussion of the legal points of the question, and am obliged when in sight of a mother wailing over the loss of her child to look upon them as persons not things. . . .

As regard my serving here, instead of elsewhere, in my letter applying for ser-vice, I made no terms and simply went where I was ordered if my relations per-sist in this unholy rebellion. I am only doing a duty to my country, which should be higher than that even to my family, in assisting to put it down. One is to affect all time, the other only my generation which will soon pass away. . . .

Love to Harriet, and all at home, and believe me

Your Aff Bro
P. Drayton

> *At the end of the war, many Confederate troops, including Thomas Dray-ton, were financially and emotionally devastated by the South's defeat. Union soldiers had burned Thomas's house to the ground, and he had spiraled into bankruptcy. Upon hearing of his brother's plight, Percival sent him money and attempted to repair the breach between them. Thomas was also ready to bury old wounds, and in a four-page letter dated July 31, 1865, he wrote with heartfelt emotion to Percival, "I am glad to see your hand writing once more, and I pray Almighty God that we may never be again so unfortunate as to be upon different sides. . . . I agree with you in thinking that we should 'set the past in the past.' "*

It is not known, however, if Percival ever received the letter or knew his brother's sentiments; Percival died of natural causes four days after it was written.

⌖ Civil War Soldier Joseph Cotton Describes to His Daughter, Mary, the Aftermath of a Terrible Battle

The war that most Northerners and Southerners thought would be decided after the first major clash proved to be the bloodiest in the nation's history; with an estimated 500,000 fatalities, almost as many Americans died in the Civil War as in all other U.S. conflicts combined. Those who saw the fighting firsthand were stunned by its ferocity. Little is known about the soldier who wrote the following missive (the letter was found tucked inside a Bible in a Methodist church in Missouri), except for his name—Joseph Cotton—and the information provided in the letter itself. In a few short lines, however, the soldier vividly conveys the ghastly image of a battlefield after combat and emphasizes that, despite all he has seen, his faith remains. The letter is dated August 9, 1861.

Camp at Cheat Mountain Pass

Miss Mary E. Cotton

My dear sweet little daughter I received both of your nice good letters and never was more delighted over any letters I ever received. Pa thought just this way, now aint it a happy thought to have a little daughter to love him as my dear little Mary loves me & aint it nice to have so little a girl as she is write her Pa so good a letter Pa has them both put away & will keep them if he can as long as he livs You must write to Pa often.

You said I must tell you all about the war. Well Pa has seen a great deal of the war since he left home he saw the battlefield just after the fight he saw 250 dead men at once he saw 200 just thrown into some deep holes all piled in on top of one another without any coffins he saw men's arms, and hands cut off & scattered around on the ground—he has seen hundreds of poor sick men lying about on the ground in tents don't you feel sorry for these poor soldiers?

Pa goes all around among the soldiers and talks to them about the Saviour & prays with them & gives them good tracts and papers to read We are now en-camped right in the midst of tall mountains which would look very strange to you they look like they reach clear up into the sky These days the mountains are now covered with ripe whortleberrys which are very nice the people bring them to our camp & we buy them & our Irishman that cooks for us makes pies for us

You must be a good girl mind Ma & pray for Pa Good by dear Mary

Pa

☞ Samuel Roosevelt Johnson Offers Words of Solace to Mrs. James Lynch After Hearing That Her Husband Has Been Killed

There is no official record of how many foreign-born troops fought in the Civil War, but some estimates put the number at one out of every ten soldiers. Immigrants from Scotland, Italy, France, Holland, Canada, Switzerland, and even Cuba all served (mostly for the North), and the largest percentage were German and Irish. Born in Donegal, Ireland, James Lynch was almost fifty years old when the Civil War began, but he still wanted to fight for the preservation of the United States. During the siege of Atlanta in the summer of 1864 by General Sherman's forces, Lynch gave his life for the country he considered his new home. Upon hearing the news of his death, a family friend named Samuel Roosevelt Johnson reflected on Lynch's faith and devotion in a letter to Mrs. Lynch, whom he knew was overcome with grief.

Bainbridge, Chenango County, N.Y.
Aug. 10, 1864

My Dear Mrs Lynch,

I read in the paper the death of Mr. James Lynch, in the Army of the Southwest and in Gen. Hooker's Division; who fell nobly daring, at the front of the Great Conflict at Atlanta, pierced by nine balls, five of which went through his heart.

I fear, nay I feel almost sure, it must be your dear husband—and that God in his mysterious Providence called you to bear this great bereavement. My dear friend—it is God's Sovereign will—and we must bow in submission when our own time comes, or the time of those we love, and must still hold fast our faith in Him. "Though he slay me yet will I trust in Him!"

It must ever be a comfort to you to recall your husband's words, how he said that we were in the hands of the Lord, and that no one of us knew where danger lay—that he had been safe in the midst of desperate battles, while his near friend, and connection had died by an accident at home.

And when we kneeled in your parlor in prayer and committed him and all our interests to the Lord, both as to body and soul, hoping in our Redeemer who came to save us poor feeble and sinful creatures, it must be a comfort to remember these Christian exercises, and his sincere and Christian interest in them. God grant His Blessing and Salvation to us all. And I pray that His Consolations may abound; and that you and your dear children in Your affliction may find your Saviour to be indeed a very present Helper, strengthener and Comforter, and very near to you.

Believe me most truly

Your sympathizing friend
Samuel Roosevelt Johnson.

Private John Ross Wallar, Dying from Wounds Sustained in Combat, Pens a Final Letter to His Loved Ones

While many troops prayed to God to see them through the war unharmed, they were well aware that His will is sometimes unknowable. Private John R. Wallar was shot in the leg and languished in a military hospital for weeks in the early fall of 1864 before succumbing to his injuries. (Civil War hospitals were so unsanitary that a soldier could arrive with a minor flesh wound and die from infections soon after being admitted.) Wallar had volunteered for the army at the age of fifteen, and he began his service as a drummer boy. He was still a teenager when he dictated a short letter home from his hospital bed in Nashville, Tennessee.

Dear Sister father Mother and friends

I recievd your letter But I don't think I Ever shall see another that you write this is Friday night But I don't think I will Live to See Morning But My Kind friends I am a Soldier of Christ I will Meet you all in Heven My Leg Has Bin taking of above My nee I am Dying at this time so don't Morn after Me fore I Have Bleed and died fore My Country May God Help you all to pray fore Me I want you all to Meet Me in Heven above Dear Sister you wanted to Know if My Leg would be Stiff God Bless Your Soul Sister I will be Stiff all over be four twenty four ours My wound Dresser is writing this Letter fore Me when you get this Letter write to Alexander Nelan fore I wont Live till Moring so good By My friends May God be with you all good by God Bless My poor Soul

John Ross Wallar, and his last letter to his family

Mary Custis, Wife of the General Robert E. Lee, Expresses to a Cousin Her Sorrow That "Almighty God [Has Not Crowned] Our Exertions with Success"

"My concern is not whether God is on our side," President Abraham Lincoln famously stated. "My greatest concern is to be on God's side, as God is always right." For the Confederate troops who thought that they had, indeed, been on the side of God during the Civil War, the capitulation of Robert E. Lee's forces to Ulysses S. Grant on April 9 (Palm Sunday), 1865, was traumatic beyond words. After the official surrender was signed, Lee told his hungry, fatigued, and brokenhearted troops to "go home now" and become "good citizens" to their country, which was soon to be reunited again. But the idea of reconciliation came harder to Robert E. Lee's wife, Mary Custis, who blamed the Union for "starving out" the South in order to achieve its war aims. She understood, however, that the outcome was final and that only God could know the reasons why the conflict ended as it had. In a short letter to her cousin Mary, Mrs. Lee articulated her thoughts in more detail and reported how her husband and their sons Fitzhugh and Robert—who had both served in the war—were faring. (There is no salutation to the letter, and her mention of "our President" is a reference to Jefferson Davis and not, needless to say, Abraham Lincoln.)

I have just heard my dear cousin Mary of an opportunity to write to tell you that we are all well as usual and thru' the mercy of God all spared thru' the terrible ordeal thru' which we have passed—I feel that I could have blessed God if those who were prepared had filled a soldiers grave. I blessed Him that they are spared I trust for a future usefulness to their poor unhappy country. My little Rob has not yet come in but we have reason to think he is safe.

Tho' it has not pleased Almighty God to crown our exertions with success in the way & manner we expected yet we must still trust & pray not that our will but His may be done in Heaven & in earth. . . .

For my part it will always be a source of pride & consolation to me to know that all mine have risked their lives fortune & even fame for so holy a cause—We can hear nothing certain from our President—may God bless & protect them—we can only pray for them—our plans are all unsettled.

Gen'l Lee is very busy getting up his army matters & then we shall probably go to some of those empty places in the vicinity of the White House. Fitzhugh has gone down there to see what he can do but that place is an utter scene of desolation—so is our whole country & the cruel policy of the enemy has accomplished its work to well. They have achieved by starvation what they could never win by their valor & nor have they taken a single town in the South except Vicksburg that we have not evacuated. Dear Cousin write me about you all & how you manage to exist would that I were able to help you. I do not think we shall be here very long therefore unless you can write at once you had better wait till you hear from me again.

The girls & the General write in love. He is wonderfully well considering all he has endured. Nanny South's wife is fine & several of her boys who have come in—Love to all friends.

Ever affectionately yours,
M C Lee

⊷⊷ **John M. Allen, Stationed at an Army
Camp in El Paso, Texas, Tells His Fiancée,
Margaret, of the Town's Wickedness and
Affirms His Devotion for Her**

*When the United States declared war on Germany in April 1917 and mil-
lions of U.S. troops were mobilized to fight overseas, the loved ones of these
servicemen were understandably concerned for the physical well-being of
their boys. But they worried about their spiritual welfare as well; they
knew that even the most moral young man could find himself seduced by
certain vices when far from home. Born in Michigan in 1896, John M.
Allen dropped out of college to enlist in the U.S. Army in 1916. Before heading to France in 1918, Allen was stationed in El Paso, Texas, a place he
deemed considerably more licentious than his hometown of Grand Rapids.
Allen wrote the following letter to his sweetheart, Margaret Belknap, to
assure her that despite the temptations around him, he would not yield
to sin. (The ellipses are in the original.)*

My guardian angel:

Of all the royal letters that come to me out of the North . . . I do not know what
would come of me without those rays of light from my home country, those frag-
ile bonds that hold me safe. I have come to call this region bad and black and all

the rest white . . . for many weeks I have seen nothing but vice and striving after vice. Soldiers were always the same, for there is that in their very position that makes them "eat, drink, and be merry" for tomorrow we may get a slug in the heart. You cannot imagine the internal wickedness of the camp, and this abetting city of the desert; and I have no reason to tell you of it except to remind you better of my love for my own girl.

Sat. night I scoured with a gang the dens and dives of the river bank. I kidded the painted ladies in the doorways. I leaned on the sloppy bars of the toughest saloons in Texas, my identity lost in the uniform of a million men. But for a reason I did not lose my identity. I did not touch a hand of the honey voiced girls of the brilliant doorways, or the handle of the mugs of the mahogany bars. I had not completely forgotten. I do not know how it was exactly, but I guess I could not lose my way in the full light of day. I may sometime be eternally grateful to you merely for the legacy of your memory. You ask what of the wives and sweethearts. A thing to conjure by for some: a dark lantern for others. It is bad.

I stood on the mt. this Sunday morning, and saw the shining Rio Grande winding thru the prairie between green banks and rows of majestic cottonwoods. On one side of the little river, Juarez, and the Mexican barracks; on the other, the big American camp and El Paso—at sword's points awaiting the issue of events in the brains of 3 or 4 men in Washington. God grant that the decisions of these brains shall be guided only by the honor they profess, and we shall follow their bidding thru hell.

I wish to send you a long kiss, for I love you and you only. John

Allen returned to Margaret, and they married in 1921. For his courage in action, Allen received the Croix de Guerre and was cited by General John Pershing for gallantry.

In a Letter to His Pastor Back Home, Private Walter Bromwich Questions God's Purpose in a Time of War

The sense of excitement with which so many troops had left the United States in 1917 and 1918 to fight in the "Great Adventure," as they referred to World War I, was quickly tempered by the sheer slaughter they encountered. Machine guns, flamethrowers, tanks, airplanes, poison gas, and other "advances" in warfare had made it possible for armies to wipe out thousands of men in a single day. Confronted with so much bloodshed, some soldiers began to reconsider their idealism and even their faith. In a short letter to his pastor back in Pennsylvania, a young private named Walter Bromwich laid out the questions he was grappling with, particularly God's role in a spectacle so terrible as warfare.

Dear Reverent:

Here I sit in my little home on the side of the hill thinking of the little church back home, wondering how you are getting along. Don't think I am down-hearted because I am writing you, but it's a queer thing I can't explain, that ever since I volunteered I've felt like a cog in a huge wheel. The cog may get smashed up, but the machine goes on, and I know I share in the progress of that machine whether I live or die, and that seems to make everything all right. Except, perhaps, when I lose a pal, it's generally one of the best but yet it may be one of the worst. And I can't feel God is in it.

How can there be fairness in one man being maimed for life, suffering agonies, another killed instantaneously, while I get out of it safe? Does God really love us individually or does He love His purpose more? Or is it better to believe he makes the innocent suffer for the guilty and that things will be squared up some day when those who have escaped suffering here will suffer, and those who have suffered here will escape suffering. Sounds rather calculating, doesn't it, and not a bit like the love of a Father.

What I would like to believe is that God is in this war, not as a spectator, but backing up everything that is good in us. He won't work any miracles for us because that would be helping us to do the work He's given us to do on our own. I don't know whether God goes forth with armies but I do know that He is in lots of our men or they would not do what they do.

Do write me and let me know how the church is getting along.

Remember me to all—especially The Altar Guild, and tell them to "carry on" the war work. My motto is "carry on." So here's good-luck to all.

Yours sincerely,
Pvt. Walter T. Bromwich
Company A 6th U. S. Engineers American Expeditionary Forces

Four months after writing this letter, Bromwich was shot in both the back and the head during combat. After extensive hospitalization, he recovered fully from his wounds.

American Red Cross Nurse Maude B. Fisher Sends Words of Comfort to the Mother of a Young Soldier Who Died After the Armistice Was Signed

At the eleventh hour on the eleventh day of the eleventh month, the war was over. Cities and towns throughout France, Germany, Russia, Great Britain, the United States, and many other nations exploded with joy on November 11, 1918, when the peace was announced. But for countless families around the globe, that happiness quickly turned to despair when they learned that their loved one had survived the war only to die from the horrific influenza pandemic that was claiming tens of millions of lives worldwide. One of these victims was a young American soldier named Richard Hogan, who became sick and then passed away just days after victory had been declared. Knowing that Hogan's mother would re-

ON ACTIVE SERVICE

with the

AMERICAN EXPEDITIONARY FORCE

AMERICAN RED CROSS

November 29th, 1918.

My dear Mrs. Hogan:-

If I could talk to you I could tell ~~you so much better about~~
your son's last sickness, and all the little things that mean so
much to a mother far away from her boy.

Your son was brought to this hospital on the 13th of November
very sick with what they called Influenza. This soon developed into
Pneumonia. He was brave and cheerful though, and made a good fight
with the disease. Several days he seemed much better, and seemed to
enjoy some fruit that I brought him. He did not want you to worry
about his being sick, but I told him I thought we ought to let you
know, and he said all right.

He became very weak towards the last of his sickness and slept
all the time. One day while I was visiting some of the other patients
he woke up and seeing me with my hat on asked the orderly if I was his
sister come to see him. He was always good and patient and the nurses
loved him. Everything was done
suffered very little, if any pai

He laughed and talked t
was able. They wanted to move
real sick and moved the new bed
that he didn't want to move.
"Come on, Hogan," he said, "Move
than the one you're in." But

"No", he said, "No, I'l
ter than mine, you'd 'a' had it

The last time I saw hi
he was too weak to do anything b

The Chaplain saw him a
he breathed his last on November

He was laid to rest in
sleeps under a simple white wood
him, have died for their country
His aluminum identification tag
around his neck, both bearing hi

- 2 -

The Plot of the grave in the cemetery where your son
is buried was given to the Army for our boys and the people of
Commercy will always tend it with loving hands and keep it fresh
and clean. I enclose here a few leaves from the grass that
grows near in a pretty meadow.

A big hill overshadows the place and the sun was setting
behind it just as the Chaplain said the last prayer over your boy.

He prayed that the people at home might have great
ength now for the battle that is before them, and we do ask that
you now.

The country will always honor   boy, because he gave
fe for it, and it will also lov   r you for the gift
boy, but be assured, it is not in vain, and
ld is better today   th

deepest sympathy
rrow.

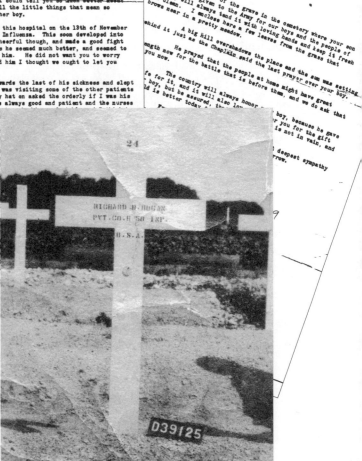

ceive only a brief telegram from the government stating that her boy was dead, an American Red Cross nurse named Maude B. Fisher sent Mrs. Hogan a more personal message. Although not overtly about faith, Fisher's letter is the very embodiment of compassion and kindness.

November 29th, 1918.

My dear Mrs. Hogan:

If I could talk to you I could tell you so much better about your son's last sickness, and all the little things that mean so much to a mother far away from her boy.

Your son was brought to this hospital on the 13th of November very sick with what they called Influenza. This soon developed into Pneumonia. He was brave and cheerful though, and made a good fight with the disease. Several days he seemed much better, and seemed to enjoy some fruit that I brought him. He did not want you to worry about his being sick, but I told him I thought we ought to let you know, and he said all right.

He became very weak towards the last of his sickness and slept all the time. One day while I was visiting some of the other patients he woke up and seeing me with my hat on asked the orderly if I was his sister come to see him. He was always good and patient and the nurses loved him. Everything was done to make him comfortable and I think he suffered very little, if any pain.

He laughed and talked to the people around him as long as he was able. They wanted to move him to another bed after he became real sick and moved the new bed up close to his, but he shook his head, that he didn't want to move. The orderly, a fine fellow, urged him. "Come on, Hogan," he said, "Move to this new bed. It's lots better than the one you're in." But Hogan shook his head still.

"No", he said, "No, I'll stay where I am. If that bed was better than mine, you'd 'a' had it long ago."

The last time I saw him I carried him a cup of hot soup, but he was too weak to do anything but taste it, and went back to sleep.

The Chaplain saw him several times and had just left him when he breathed his last on November 25th, at 2:30 in the afternoon.

He was laid to rest in the little cemetery of Commercy, and sleeps under a simple white wooden cross among his comrades who, like him, have died for their country. His grave is number 22, plot 1. His aluminum identification tag is on the cross, and a similar one is around his neck, both bearing his serial number, 2793346.

The plot of the grave in the cemetery where your son is buried was given to the Army for our boys and the people of Commercy will always tend it with loving hands and keep it fresh and clean. I enclose here a few leaves from the grass that grows near in a pretty meadow.

A big hill overshadows the place and the sun was setting behind it just as the Chaplain said the last prayer over your boy.

He prayed that the people at home might have great strength now for the battle that is before them, and we do ask that for you now.

The country will always honor your boy, because he gave his life for it, and it will also love and honor you for the gift of your boy, but be assured, that the sacrifice is not in vain, and the world is better today for it.

From the whole hospital force, accept deepest sympathy and from myself, tenderest love in your hour of sorrow.

Sincerely,
Maude B. Fisher

Lieutenant David A. Thompson, Working with the American Graves Registration Service, Describes to His Father How Overwhelming It Was to Find and Identify the Body of a Certain Fallen Soldier

Some of the most moving sights any American traveling abroad will ever see are the military cemeteries that hold the graves of U.S. troops who sacrificed their lives so that others could be free. The image of these immac-

ulate grounds covered with row after row of white crosses is especially heartrending when one considers how far away these fallen heroes are from their homes in the States. Instead, they are buried side by side with their brothers in arms near the battlefields where they were killed. At the conclusion of World War I, the American Graves Registration Service was tasked with finding the bodies of slain U.S. troops throughout Europe and interring them properly. For the servicemen involved with this effort, the assignment could be a difficult one, both physically and emotionally. And for a twenty-seven-year-old Army lieutenant from Massachusetts named David Arthur Thompson, the job was intensely personal as well; one of the bodies he helped recover was that of Joseph Thompson—his own brother. David wrote about the experience in an astonishingly candid but also very poignant letter to his father dated May 24, 1919.

Dear Dad,

I intended to write mother, but I can't tell her as much as I can you. When you read this, you can explain to her everything that you wish.

I have just taken Joe from his grave in the woods to a lot in the national American Cemetery at Romagne, France. I had to supervise the work myself on account of the shortage of officers; therefore, made a personal inspection of the body, which as you might know, I'd rather die than do, but which had to be done.

I'm going to be very plain in telling you, and know it might hurt, but I know you will wish to know. I am awful glad that it was I that could do it, and not any of you, as it would have drove any of you insane.

With three colored boys given me as a detail and a Dodge light truck, I made my way over the hills 40 miles. Sometimes the road was so bad we had to cross fields, and at one place had to build a small bridge over a place where the road was destroyed.

We left Romagne at 7:30 and got to the grave at the Harmont woods at noon. I had the colored fellows dig down the side of the grave until we struck the body, or could see the clothes. I saw his feet and legs first, and then the rest of his body, just as he fell.

He was dressed in new clothes, and had on his rain coat, and full pack, with the exception of the rifle and helmet. He was not in a box, as I expected, but merely a blanket thrown over the top of his body, and some loose boards over that. We removed the blanket, boards, etc. And of course, the body was badly decomposed. . . . I then unbuttoned the coats and found his other identification tag about his neck, which then and there identified him without going further.

I then placed him in a coffin we had brought with us and placed it in the car. We then got the body of Carl Coombs out, as we did Joe. Coombs' body was also badly decomposed, and he was a heavy boy to lift out. . . .

We then had both bodies in the car and drove back to Romagne by going away around through the rear of the German lines, and got back to the cemetery at Romagne about 5:00 p.m. There I turned both bodies over the undertakers who were present. I had the clothes removed and carefully searched, with good results.

I found in his clothes: your last letter to him, a pocket knife, fountain pen, his diary, testament, Book of Psalms, another book with annotations of all mail received and sent, some small pictures he had received from home, about 10 Francs in money, two watches, one his own, the other a German watch, a few German coins, and German post cards.

His diary is very interesting, and his Psalm book is wonderful, and shows that he died with a clean soul. This little book is known as, "The Shepherd Psalm", and was given to him by Emily M. Rogers. In it he has written a little prayer which is as follows:

"I pray thee, O God, that I may be beautiful within. This is my most earnest prayer. Most of us I believe will see home and friends again. If we do, how many will curse every drink they have taken, every oath they have uttered, every shameful thing they have committed here, that they wouldn't at home.

It threatens my stripes, my discipline, my popularity, and my advancement. These four things are temporary. The clean within is permanent and is greater than all of these temporal things.

David A. Thompson

This war will last but a short time. I have 30 to 1 chances of coming out. What is one year of service to indulgence, to say, 50 years and one year of service; and a clean conscience for the other 50 years. Anyway, after, before, present, or anytime, I despise all ungodly things. My real inner self resents it. . . ."

Now, Dad, isn't that most wonderful. I wish you would tell Dr. Day of it. There are many other smaller verses, all of great interest. On the last day of the diary, written October 14th, as he was leaving Verdun, for the Harmont, he writes as follows:

"Oh, it's hard to realize peace when the shells of the enemy are tearing all around us. "Peace" Oh! I pray God it will come before morning, and Mother's prayer may be realized. . . ."

The poor kid prayed for peace and God gave it to him, Dad. How thankful I am that God gave it instantly. He was prepared to die, and did not suffer. I am happy over the thoughts of it, but God only knows how I miss him. I loved him so much.

Dad, these things are worth the world to you. I shall preserve them carefully; although they are in pretty bad shape, owing to the dampness of the ground and body. Also, they are badly stained and smell bad. I have soaked them all in gasoline, and in a day or so, they will be O.K. . . .

Joe now rests beside Carl Coombs in the Romagne Cemetery, with 35,000 others. It is a beautiful place and our national Monument in France. I pray that you will let his body lie there in peace. I know he would wish it.

He is now buried deep in a coffin; and on Memorial Day, his grave will be beautifully decorated. General Pershing will be there to pay his last respects to his men who fought under him and it will be a beautiful ceremony. . . . As I stay over here longer, and see how well our cemeteries here will be taken care of, I am more convinced that our Joe should remain here. I have had one experience of moving his body, and it was so hard that I wish now that you all would allow it to remain here as a part of our country's great monument to the world war.

They have started a movement in France to have some girl look after each grave, or group of graves. There is a young girl here that will look after them both, that is, Joe's and Carl Coombs'. She is the only girl that has ever visited their graves. She went there only under great risk and hardships. Just because she wanted to be the one that could have charge of the graves after we are all gone. She wrote to Ma and as she speaks and writes very good English, I know Ma will be glad to write her in the years to come. As this girl has the time and means to go there, she will do it gladly. She has been reading Joe's diary, and Psalm book, and I tell you, it is enough to impress anyone. They have been very good friends to me here.

I know Ma will be pleased to have this stuff. To see his own writing will be more to her than his body. Please let it now Rest in Peace.

I feel now that I have accomplished everything possible. The grave location is: Section 9, Plot 3, Grave 155. Joe is buried in the <u>Northeast corner</u>.

Write soon, Dad, and love to all.

Your Son, Art.

⇒⇥ **In 1933, Alexander Goode Writes to His Sweetheart, Theresa Flax, About a Growing Threat to World Peace—a Man Named Adolf Hitler**
&
Goode, Weeks Before His Legendary Act of Heroism, Assures Theresa of His Love for Her

Only months after the end of World War I, a young Austrian veteran of the conflict named Adolf Hitler became the chief propagandist for the National Socialist German Workers Party, which blamed most of Germany's problems on Jews. Hitler was named president of the organization, better known as the Nazi Party, in 1920, and he swiftly gained national prominence by preying on the Germans' postwar humiliation. Thirteen years later he was appointed chancellor of Germany. Although most Americans were understandably preoccupied with the Great Depression at the time, many Jews in the States were closely watching Hitler and his rabid anti-Semitism. They knew that German Jews were being harassed and persecuted and that Hitler's rhetoric was becoming increasingly fanatical. Twenty-three-year-old rabbinical student Alexander Goode was well aware of Hitler's ominous rise to power, and in a letter to his sweetheart, Theresa Flax, he predicted how dangerous Hitler would be—not only to Jews, but to Germany itself. The letter, dated April 3, 1933, was written more than six and a half years before the start of World War II. (The long ellipses are in the original.)

Rabbi Alexander Goode

Darling. . . .

Theresa, dear, why don't you write me sometime more intimately about yourself, what your opinion on things is, what you think about, what your interests are, anything at all so that I can feel I am closer to you when I read your letters, something that will reveal you yourself, in all your charm and sweetness, just say anything at all as long as it concerns you and I will love it. . . . . . .

Recently I have cultivated a taste for poetry, a sure sign that I have become a mere shadow of my stern self and now am as sentimental and love-smitten as all the fellows I used to laugh at in former years. Keats and Shelley are my high-brow recreations now and fine fare they are too. If it were not for my infernal habit of reading so terrifically fast I could no doubt appreciate far more their charm and beauty. It is not at all mushy either. Perhaps when I become more familiar with them I'll try to impart some of the joy I get from reading their poetry to you. The Bible is not so bad for poetry either. Just read the Song of Songs sometime. It is not long, but its beauty is overpowering. They are the lovesongs of the ancient Hebrews and as love poetry they have never been surpassed.

Speaking of the Bible I might mention that by this time in my preparation for the career of a Rabbi I have read most of the Bible, and when I say read I really mean studied carefully, at least three times, so that I am more familiar with this great library of our people than I am with any other volume I have ever studied or read. In it is stored such a mine of information and beauty that I am tempted to think with our ancestors who absolutely believed that everything in the Bible was true and that all things that man can experience under the sun are contained therein. So much is treasured up that I could not begin to describe its contents.

It really is heartrending that more people do not seek out its treasures. Perhaps if Hitler read some of its valuable sayings he would be a wiser ruler than he is destined to become.

His policy now means utter ruin, not only to the Jews, but to the whole of Germany itself. He can no more injure the Jews of Germany without seriously depriving the nation itself of all its wealth and position than he can cut off his nose without detriment to his Charlie Chaplinesque physiognomy. I see no hope for our kinsmen abroad. Germany's loss, however, is our gain for expulsion of the Jews from Germany means that many of the greatest Jews alive today will emigrate to America and greatly promote the development of Jewish culture in this country. As long as their lives are not injured it will be a gain to American Jewry to have these Jews here. There should be no difficulty in the way of their entering America. This country will be glad to have them.

There I go veering off at a tangent. I am grateful to this letter indeed because it has caught my interest and made me lose sight of my own mood, blue as blue can be, of an hour ago. I think I feel better now. May my slumber be as peaceful as I hope yours will be tonight . . . so with a tender caress . . . . . goodnight. Alex

In 1934, Alexander Goode and Theresa Flax married. Four years later they had a baby daughter, Rosalie Bea. An extremely patriotic young man, Goode had volunteered for the National Guard in high school, and, when war was declared in December 1941, he enlisted in the U.S. Army. After completing his orientation at Harvard University's Chaplain School, Rabbi Goode, age thirty-two, was ready to deploy overseas. Right before he embarked for Europe in early January 1943 on a troopship named the USAT Dorchester, *he quickly wrote a letter to Theresa.*

Darling:

Just a hurried line as I rush my packing. I'll be on my way in an hour or two. I got back yesterday afternoon just before the warning. Hard as it was for us to say goodbye in N. Y. at least we could see each other before I left.

Don't worry—I'll be coming back much sooner than you think.

Left to right: Fr. John Washington, Reverend George Fox, and Reverend Clark Poling

Take care of yourself and the baby—a kiss for each of you. I'll keep thinking of you.

Remember I love you very much. Alex

These were the last words Theresa Goode ever received from her husband. At 1:00 a.m. on February 3, 1943, the Dorchester *was torpedoed one hundred miles off the coast of Greenland by a German submarine. As soldiers aboard the sinking ship began to panic, Goode, along with three other chaplains—George Fox (Methodist), John Washington (Catholic), and Clark Poling (Dutch Reformed)—did everything they could to calm the frightened men and help the wounded put on their life jackets. But only minutes later they made a horrendous discovery: There weren't enough life preservers for everyone on board. According to eyewitnesses, once the chaplains made this realization, they quickly removed their own preservers— which meant they would almost certainly drown—and gave them to the first soldiers they could find. The last anyone saw of the chaplains was*

the four men, locked arm in arm, praying together as the ship went down,
taking them and 672 other men to their graves in the icy waters of the At-
lantic. The bodies of the chaplains were never found.

An American Serviceman Describes to His Mother in Harrowing Detail What Happened When His Ship Was Attacked

Very little personal information is known about the writer of the follow-
ing letter—the original copy ended up in the hands of someone with no
connection to the man's family—except that he endured a terrifying or-
deal while at sea. But even in the most dire circumstances imaginable, he
firmly held on to his faith. (There is no signature to the letter, and the
blank spaces indicate where it was edited by military censors.)

September 29, 1942

Dearest Mother:

Don't think I'll have an opportunity to mail this to you and even if I did it would probably take months and be strictly censored, but I do want to let you know what's happened and what I've been thinking about the last little bit. Know you've probably done a lot of worrying because you haven't heard from me in a long time. Well Mother—your son's a survivor. Yes, now I know how it feels to lay in a life boat and on a raft for long long days and nights. The story actually starts about a week and a day after we left Halifax. It was Sunday. The day was warm for an ordinary North Atlantic Day in Mid-Winter. . . .

Things went quiet for a while then there was a big storm. Waves three times the height of the ship rose and fell, luckily not too many breaking on us. The convoy Commander decided to head the Convoy into the storm to try and ride out of it. Our ship was never built for such weather and was in no condition at the time to do it. Our deck cargo was becoming loose from the rolling of the ship. We kept on with the storm but next day it had not abated, and we tried to turn but snapped our steering cable. Late that afternoon it was repaired. The next day we turned again and in the late afternoon we turned again and managed to ride the storm a little better.

All the thinking I tried to do during that storm. Sea sickness is just mental—I thought. From Sunday until Wednesday I couldn't hold anything. Kept trying to say that the rainbow that I could see in the spray meant for us as God promised Noah, that the storm would soon be over. By Sunday night the merchant crew and the gun crew quarters were awash back aft. So they all packed into the captains' room, the mates and everyone else, including our two by four shack, which I kept thinking would be washed off the deck.

Living conditions up until that time were bearable but these new conditions made them miserable. I feel quite confident that if I'm ever assigned to another ship quite like the   I'll resign and join the Navy or the Coast Guard. The money and officers' uniform are attractive and shiney but they aren't worth it. Our alley ways were three to four inches deep in water, the mess boys were sick and frightened and refused to work. I had sprained my ankle a day or two before all this happened and between my incessant wretching and the pain, was really feeling low.

Monday night the little kid in the gun crew who had gotten put in jail in Halifax for disturbing the peace, was washed overboard. The ship even lacked line enough to throw to him. The boys that were on deck with him all hoped that he was knocked unconscious but the cold water probably brought him to. They say his hand was stretched up in the air for help but nothing could be done for him. The storm was too rough for us to risk the boat to save him. Losing him had a strange effect on the crew.

Wednesday the eventful day, September twenty-third—in the afternoon a sub fired two shells at us. The first fell short and the second ran under us as we rode a wave. We fired our 4" gun, aft (not much ammunition was left for it because of water getting into the storeroom) and thought we came real close to the sub. By now we were not in sight of a ship. Then at 9:53 when I was on watch we were hit. I had just rushed up to the ice machine to get some cold water and continued on up when hearing the alarm. We had lost our port lifeboat, and two rafts in the storm, leaving just the starboard life boat and two rafts.

Because I had a rubber suit on I was supposed to get on a life raft and the gun crew were to get into the lifeboat. I got in as far as the lifeboat but couldn't see the rafts and jumped into the boat. No one was practised enough and all too excited to do a good job. Someone cut the falls allowing the boat to drop into the water. It's strange, the boat that leaked when we left New York was the one that was not taken by the storm.

There was much confusion, the boat overloaded, and the plug had been put in, and the skipper was giving a fast stroke. We finally got away from the ship, which took seventeen minutes to go down. We found the other two life rafts. There were only two missing, one able bodied seaman and a mess boy. The A.B. Seaman was crushed between a raft and the hull of the ship, the mess boy was pulled aft and into the propeller blades.

As we watched her go down some laughed, some cried. One little wiper on a raft was in such bad shape he had no control over himself and just shook violently. The last minute before she sank the fog whistle blew first a couple of times faintly and then at last real lustily.

Writing this is like living it all over again. Before we abandoned ship Sparks had sent three SOS's, the last one was acknowledged. The next day when no help came we thought it may have been the sub that acknowledged the message, but now looking back it couldn't have been.

When I went over I thought I had just about everything I wanted real badly but now think of small things I could have taken. All I had under my rubber suit was a set of work clothes, pair of woolen socks, two sweat shirts, two sweaters (one of which Mrs. Van Buren knitted). In the water proof pocket I had my pen and pencil, papers and wallet. Forgot my flashlight and had no gloves.

Those next sixty hours I hope never to have to go through again. The next morning the men on the rafts were taken into the boat and we in the life boat went on the rafts. We stayed on the rafts all day and night, then the next day even though the water was rough we managed to transfer again. On the raft we were comfortable but water washed over us and there was no way to break the wind. There was enough food but we wanted to ration it, not knowing how long we'd be out. I couldn't figure which was more uncomfortable being on the raft cold and damp or in the life boat cramped and uncomfortable but a little warmer. Bailing had to be kept up continually and some of the men really turned out to be heels and others heroes. I was still vomiting. We'd been given a little piece of chocolate, a couple of malted milk tablets and a little water each day. One of the damned mess boys got my half of a package of graham crackers and ate them. I didn't care much though because I only tossed it up as soon as it went down. Finally I came to the point where I didn't have anything to toss.

Thoughts going through my mind those hours sure were something to note. Mostly my thoughts sought God. I thought lots of you saying you were being brave over the phone, of you going to readings, of Aunt Florence, her faith, the Lord's Prayer, and the twenty-third Psalm. I'd wonder if I'd ever walk through Goldsmiths again and pass the counter where they sold Malted Milk Tablets. Thought of you reading the article in the Digest about those men on a raft for so many days, but then they weren't in the North Atlantic at a pretty cold season of the year. Things seemed pretty desperate the next day when no help came from Sparks SOS. The gulls in the sky looked like planes, then at night in the raft the lifeboat looked like a distant tanker.

I kept trying to keep faith in God and remember that whatever was, was His will. It really helped me a lot. Saturday Morning we sighted a ship. The skipper shot flares, attracted their attention and they came for us. It was the Coast Guard boat U.S.S.   on which I'm writing this account. The crew and all have treated us swell. We were in the lifeboats and on rafts 60 hours and when we boarded the   it was as tho we were in a dream, warm clothes, warm shower, and good soup and coffee.

Staff Sergeant George Syer, Just Before Shipping Off to Fight, Realizes That He Might Not Return Alive and Leaves Behind a Letter for His Infant Son

For servicemen and women embarking overseas, saying good-bye to loved ones is heartbreaking enough, but for troops who are parents, it can be especially difficult to leave behind young children. An Army staff sergeant in 1st Headquarters Company, 382nd Battalion, 96th Division, George Syer departed for the Pacific in late July 1944 after spending only ten days with his newborn son, John Paul, at their home in Galveston, Texas. On July 20, Syer wrote John Paul the following letter to let his son know how dearly he loved him.

Dear son;

Our son, our first born. I was happy at your coming. Happy that the Lord brought you into mother and I's realm of love. Before your coming mother and I desired you very much. Our Joy began with the first sign of your coming. We planned for you from that moment. Mother agreed that if you come I should be the one to give you your name. I chose the name John Paul because of my hopes for you. The hope that you will accept the call of the Lord to Salvation and service. The men after whom you are named were kind and dynamic followers of the Lord. None then or since have been greater. No greater life can be lived, even though poverty and martyrdom be the lot of those that follow Jesus.

Mr. and Mrs. George Syer with their newborn son

I have the natural pride of a father and would have naturally named you George: Which was mother and grandparents desire, had not my desire to influence you to choose the way of life overcome my parental pride.

I arrived three days after your birth, then! only because the Lord made it possible, in answer to our prayers. A nation at war doesnt allow its soldiers many priviledges.

Ten days, mother, you and I were together. Days in which I learned to take care of you, mother at that time being not strong enough. Mother and I loved you with out reserve during those days. Examined each part of you and watched every little change in your growth.

Then came that day when I was to go leaving mother to be both mother and dad to you. It was hard on mother when I left, but she bore bravely the seperation. One of my hardest farewell was to bend and kiss you good by son. Then I was gone, speeding back to California to take up my duties again as a soldier of my country

Two months have gone now since you were born. Mother has since sent pictures that I treasure. You are a goodly child such as the child of a Levi parent recorded in the Scriptures

Yes two months, and tonight I am on the threshold of another adventure of life. Tomorrow we board ship to go overseas. I do not fear to go knowing that I too must share the responsibility of fighting for my country. I have no desire to kill son only to save life, but there are time like these that one can't understand, but seek to serve God and also my country seems the only true course to take.

I go with faith that the Lord shall bring me back safe from the conflict. However should the Lord decide that my service has ended, and I fall on foreign soil, my faith will be satisfied to its fullest by Him who is wise and better than I could ask or expect.

The answer to our faith is always complete, even though the answer is not according to your own will. A paradox, yes but that is God's priviledge and power.

Will close this letter now son, future days will bring more thoughts

Love
Your dad
George

> *Staff Sergeant Syer, who earned two Bronze Star with Valor medals during the war, returned home alive and well.*

Corporal William "Bicky" Kiessel, Fighting in Italy, Explains to Two Friends What Goes Through a Soldier's Mind Before Heading Into Combat
&
Private First Class Albert Kishler Jr. Describes to a Fellow Serviceman Who Has Not Experienced a Land Battle What It Feels Like to Be Under Fire

"This letter is for your reading only; or to others at your discretion; but under no conditions to my Mother," twenty-six-year-old Corporal William "Bicky" Kiessel wrote on November 13, 1943, to a favorite uncle who had fought in World War I. Kiessel had just survived the invasion of Italy, and he thought his uncle would understand what he had been through. *"We were the first Americans to hit Europe,"* Kiessel continued in his hastily typed letter.

> *I've been bombed, straffed, shelled, chased by tanks, sniped at, machine gunned and everything imaginable—and some not. I got knocked about, bruised and scraped but never directly hit. The closest I came to getting killed, I guess, was having a man on either side of me killed and I was completely picked up and tossed about ten feet. I got in such tight places that on two different times I lost all my equipment and had to pick up dead men's rifles, packs and canteen.*

"I could go into vivid detail but I've said too much now," Kiessel concluded. *"You'd better say a little prayer for me."* (One can understand why he thought his mother might be less than thrilled to read the letter.) Nine months later, Kiessel, who would ultimately survive the war, was preparing for another invasion—this time into France. The letter he wrote to two college friends right before the assault offers a revealing

glimpse into the thoughts and emotions of a young man about to charge into battle.

Dear Florence! And Jerry!

To you it is glorious history now. You know where, when and how we hit. I mean the Invasion, of course.

To me, now, it is still a dreaded ominous suspense. Sort of like waiting in the ante-room of a dentist. Only much worse!

Everything except our absolute essentials has been packed away in a burlap bag and stored. I've got the clothes I'm wearing plus one change of underwear and socks and toilet articles.

We are equipped now for anything and everything; our dog tags around our neck, identification card in pocket and name and serial number inside both shoes in case we come to a parting of the ways. We've been issued water proof casing for our rifle, bandolier of ammo, halcyon tablets to purify water, canned heat, a paper sack and sea sick pills. My gas mask is water proofed and I've got a knife in my belt, though I have no expectation of using it. In my combat pack (we call them come-back pack) I have rations for three days; 3 "D's" (concentrated chocolate) and 6 "K's". After that we should be able to get "O's".

The last mail in or out is over with for an undetermined period. We have all written our mothers, wives, or sweethearts our last letter for quite a while—or for ever. It was, of course, happy-go-lucky and carefree so as not to worry them or let them suspect our mission. A GI worries more about his folks worrying than he does about himself. . . .

We've separated from most of our friends. Nothing dramatic in parting but a casual "see yuh soon" or a careless "take care of yourself, fella". But we both feel the sincerity of it and respect each others "meet again" attitude.

What are our feelings—our emotions? Naturally it depends upon the individual. There is a sense of dullness to the very present. You think a lot about the past. People you know or knew and last associations, of home, though not about big things but a lot of silly little trifles or remembrances pop into your mind and if you were to stop and figure out "why?" you probably would never know. Thoughts that are precious, moments unreturnable flash past. We are different men since we have been fighting. To a great extent, unfortunately, we have lost our sensitiveness, there is a cold calculating air. We have gone through and experienced what men should not. But at times like these we are mother's sons once more.

You get to thinking about the future. The idle period of waiting is nerve wracking. Everything is ready, there is just the period of absolutely nothing to do—that is nothing to do but sleep, read, play cards, and there are always crap games going on with fabulous stakes because no one is thinking about the value of money. Small groups squat around and talk about everything but the impending crisis. The new replacements are outwardly unconcerned, making flippant remarks. The few remaining veterans of the Salerno battle are more thoughtful and quiet—but less calm. They figure their number is about up. Some of their buddies fell at Alteville and the Solo River, others got theirs storming Hill 1205 or San Pietro. They remember entire platoons and even companies wiped out at the unforgettable Rapido, cut down by "screaming meenies" and mortars or drowned horribly in the icy waters. A few more friends fell in the break through from Anzio. Velletri, Rome and Grossoto decimated the originals until the veterans who landed over eleven months ago in Italy are few—and thoughtful. Now we are to strike somewhere else—soon!

We're not yet on the boats. But I know what it will be like. I remember so clearly from the last time; iron folding cots, four tiers high and jammed so close that you can hardly pass in the narrow aisles, especially with your life belt on. Down in the holds its dark and hot and smelly with sweated unwashed bodies. There is the warm sickening stench of food. The boat is so crowded there is always a line eating and the heavy air is mixed with all sorts of odors—none of them pleasant. . . .

The energetic chaplains are busy holding services all hours of the day on the various dock levels. Fellows are trying to catch up on years of neglected religion in a few days. And it can be done—and is! The Catholics have Mass, Communion and Confessions while the Protestants preach little, pray much, and sing the favorite hymns of the Church. And then there are Jewish services for members of that faith. At all these sacred gatherings there is a sincerity and informality that makes for a better and greater fellowship and gives a deeper sense of the intangible value of friends, home, and the eternal verities of life. Were the world to live in this rare state of grace there would be no wars. In those services we all wish we'd lived better, been more complimentary and less critical, written home more lovingly and more often, etc. We are finally face to face with life; tho reality of it is so tremendous an effort. . . .

I don't pray, nor do I want others, to pray for my safety or return. That is not of prime importance. In life we too often emphasize the wrong things. We don't put first things first. We become satisfied with the good and don't press on to the best values in life. No, safety isn't the ultimate goal. But true examplary conduct is. What is important is that whatever does happen to me I will play my part as a man and do absolutely nothing that will shame my character or my God. To me the supreme words, the finist and highest commendation in the whole wide world is, "Well done thou good and faithful servant. Thou hast fought the good fight, thou hast kept the faith. Enter thou into the kingdom of Heaven."

Sorry if I seem to be getting dramatic. Don't mean to. I fully expect with God's Holy Will that I shall come through. Wanted you to know my reactions preceding this greatest of all invasions. Lets hope and pray that the lives lost will be worth it; as if any price can pay for a life. I want to get home; we all want to go home and though it will mean never for some, for most this will mean a much closer path through time to those whom we love and who love us so dearly.

Must crate the typewriter now. Was lucky to have it this long. Its late in the morning now and most of the fellows are down on the beach. Will join them and have fun and who can tell might start a seeming spontaneous song service. And so I bid you adieu. Christians never say goodbye. Sooner or later we all meet again.

Bicky

Another young soldier fighting in Europe, Private First Class Albert Kishler Jr., kept in touch with a close friend and former neighbor, Adrian Nader, who had joined the Navy but had not experienced ground combat. In a letter written to Nader over a two-day period (December 17

*and 18, 1944), Kishler described what goes through a man's mind when
the bombs and bullets actually start to fly. (A "BAR," alluded to in the letter, is a Browning Automatic Rifle.)*

Dear Adrian,

I received your November 19th letter yesterday in my foxhole and read it while the
88's and burp guns played over our positions. Your description of the Leyte invasion and the battle afterwards was most interesting. We also have seen quite a
bit of action during the past two months. I'm with the Ninth Army north of
Aachen and believe me we've really been pushing the Krauts around.

We too operate behind smoke screens but not as a comfortable range as you.
Jerry can and does throw a lot of lead at night and whenever smoke blinds him.
The SS troopers are true fanatics and there's no resting when they're around. It
takes bayonets, guts and death to convince the Nazi that he'd better turn tail. The
Poles, Austrians, and Czechs make good enemies but the German matches you
trick for trick and guts with guts.

December 18th, Sunday

Sunday—God's Day. The man who said that there are no atheists in foxholes
had hit the nail on the head. When the sun goes down and darkness steals in, life
to the infantrymen becomes nothing more than a gust of wind. The nights are
long, <u>fifteen</u> hours and cold and you are invariably dug in the middle of a sugar
beet field—Germany is all beet fields, orchards, and towns. To get back to the foxhole, there you are—a grenade in one hand, more handy, and your other hand fin-
gering your BAR—it's you and good old Mother Earth and God. And when the
time comes that you leave that hole and charge across several hundred yards of
enemy territory with machine guns burning, 88's and mortars thinning your
numbers, God is never forgotten. To us, death is no distant unknown. . . .

Several Sundays ago, just after we had completed one of our toughest battles,
the Chaplain preached a sermon that I shall never forget!—"Our God is eternally
just. Our God is eternally seeking. Our God is eternally loving.—It's easy to die
but it's difficult to go on living."

We are on the road to victory, but we are leaving a blazing trail. The "Battle Hymn of the Republic" and the 23rd Psalm are my constant companions on the Road, and home, Mildred, and peace my dream. "The wheels of justice grind slow and fine."

The candle's going out; more later.—

Albert, Jr.

Kishler would ultimately be wounded twice in battle, but he survived the war.

⌖ In a Letter to His Parents, Lieutenant James R. Penton Profiles an Individual He Encountered Who Embodied True Faith in Action

Despite the main shortcoming of letters sent through the mail—mostly, that they can take weeks and sometimes even months to reach their destination—handwritten correspondences have their own unique value. For one, they offer recipients a tangible connection to their loved ones, who can hold the actual paper that their sweetheart or child or parent also touched. They can also be embellished with drawings and other artwork, and it is not uncommon for troops to include an illustration or two in their letters home. Twenty-seven-year-old Lieutenant James R. Penton, who served in France with the 612th Tank Destroyer Battalion, 2nd Infantry Division, enjoyed drawing sketches of interesting people and places as he and his fellow soldiers pushed their way toward Germany. On September 3, 1944, Penton sent the following letter to his parents back in Philadelphia after being deeply moved by the sight of a woman who was the very epitome of grace under fire. (The unusual punctuation is in the original.)

Dear Mother and Governor:

In the "Reader's Digest" there's a monthly article entitled "The Most Unforgettable Character I've Known,"—or something of the sort. Well, not so long ago I met an unforgettable character myself . . . .

My guns were in position in a small farmyard in the recently-wrested town of Vire, along the crest of a beautiful ridge,—and but a stone's throw from the rubble-dusty-haze rising above the warm ruins of the cities' downtown business section. There was no "Business As Usual" in Vire that night,—only "Nazi-Tactics as Usual" as the Butchers of Spirit and Property harassed the town from afar with artillery shells aimed at no one spot in particular. My platoon crept into town as dusk merged into darkness,—barely moving at all in the tortured streets so as to keep down dust---and resulting enemy observation.

And as the sun of early morning dissolved the fog, yawning faces appeared from the depths of holes in the ground, and the boys were moving about comparing notes about the night before. Considerable interest was shown in the truck,—which had suffered three gashed tires, a perforated radiator, and other numerous shrapnel holes. In the light of day I noticed a sprawling, peaceful convent to the immediate rear of the position—with its courtyard and spires almost miraculously untouched. And while I sat there,—in the protection of a bank, gazing at the convent and listening to the melodious chiming of its bells intermingle with the hideous wail of Jerry 88's,—a solitary nun made her way deliberately through the yard, a bucket of water in one hand. It was a shock to hear her address me in perfect English, show identification papers, and learn that she was caring for the livestock in the absence of the terrorized farmer and his family. And that's the sum and substance of my story. All morning long, as the whine of Jerry artillery overhead kept the rest of us in our holes, that nun moved serenely and placidly about the skeleton of the burned-out barn,—and around the bodies of dead, bloated cows; ----- milking the swollen cows, feeding and watering the chickens, collecting eggs.

And I know that our most argumentative and skeptical atheist was duly fascinated and impressed by that display of the power and force of that Sister's faith——and complete fearlessness . . . . . . It was not the sudden, stimulated and short-lived courage which drives a man to risk hot lead on a daring dash to aid a buddy, to me, it was far more than that . . . . . It was the picture of a mellowed and complete faith,—it was serenity of mind and soul amidst man's savagery of arm and spirit. . . . . That nun hadn't spent two years of training, and "battle-conditioning" and crawling under gun fire . . . . . but her poise and expression

"The Nun of Vire," by James R. Penton

and dogged pursuit of someone else's domestic duties in the midst of that inferno was something we will all remember;—as we will the quarter-hourly chiming of the convent bells, as if in patient, long suffering defiance of the high explosive shells which ripped the city . . . . And as I sketched the nun,—some of the boys glanced over my shoulder . . . There was no title on the paper,—but every one immediately recollected . . .

Well, there is nothing new to say. We seem to be doing things rapidly here in France,—but don't expect that daily collapse . . . These Germans are either crazymen or madmen,—and the fact that they are being cut off into little "pockets" does not prevent their generals from driving them to the long drawn-out slaughter . . . . .

Do not worry when I don't have time to write. You know in the army—"no news is good news." Love to all, Jim

More than two months after writing this letter, Penton was shot through his right shoulder. "Well, how's this for my first southpaw letter?" he began a brief, surprisingly positive message to his parents on December 23. "My right arm is in a plaster of Paris cast,—I'm in Paris, too—France. . . . I'm O.K., though, and will soon be in England. Don't worry over me. Love to all, Jim." After returning to the States, Penton recuperated fully and continued to draw and paint.

⊂═⇥ **Combat Nurse June Wandrey Offers Her Sister Betty Her Impressions of the Vatican—and the Pope**

Twenty-two years old when she enlisted in the Army Nurse Corps, June Wandrey was five-foot-two with, in her own words, "finely honed muscles that were dynamite ready." (She signed one of her first letters to her family back in Wisconsin, "Your littlest tomboy.") Beginning in March 1943,

Wandrey served for more than two and a half years throughout North Africa and Europe as a combat nurse. The work was dangerous, often exhilarating, sometimes tedious, and, at times, even had its humorous moments. In June 1944, Wandrey went on leave to Rome and had the opportunity to see the Vatican. The visit, which she described in a letter to her older sister, turned out to be quite memorable.

6-15-44 Italy

Dear Betty,

Today was my turn to go to the Vatican; I wore my dress uniform with a skirt. I went with our Catholic chaplain. Two Catholic nurses from another hospital joined us as we were crossing the Piazza S. Piedro. The Swiss Guards wear the most colorful garb, big black tam-o-shanters, blue and black leg-o-mutton blouses, and knee breeches. They carry staffs. The men who guard the Pope have helmets with plumes, spears, and multi-colored garments on the same order as the Swiss guards. They are the Papal colors of the early Roman Empire. There were thousands of GIs at the audience with the Pope.

We stood in the front row. The Pope stopped right in front of me. He's as small as I am. I gave him a big smile and he extended his ring to me to kiss. Methodists just don't go around kissing old men's rings as you well know, so I didn't. If one thinks of the sanitary aspects of that antiquated custom, it's repulsive. Instead I extended my hand to him, gave him a happy, hearty handshake. We chatted briefly. I told him I came from Wisconsin. Also about the great fishing there and put in a good word for Father Nurnberg. Are he and Mom still discussing religions? The Pope blessed a rosary and gave it to me. I'm going to give it to Mrs. B. when I get back. It isn't safe to send things home.

Perhaps I rattled his Papal cage, but I meant no disrespect. His position I salute. The Catholic nurses on either side of me wanted to hit me over the head after it was over. They were burned up because he didn't speak to them and wasted his attention on me. They broke out a package of cigarettes and started to smoke in the Vatican. To me that was a sacrilege. The Vatican is a wonderful, incredibly beautiful building made so by the paintings and sculptures. The Judgement Day is magnificent. There must be a thousand rooms in the compound. I think even an atheist would be moved by the Holy nature of this place.

I have an infected finger from a jab with a dirty needle in the OR. The sulfadiazine I'm taking has made me absolutely sluggish and it doesn't become me.

Love, June

Wandrey returned to the United States in 1945 after receiving a total of eight battle stars for campaigns throughout North Africa and Europe.

June Wandrey

Gabriel Navarro Expresses to His Son Porfirio, Who Has Been Fighting in the Pacific for One Year, How Proud He Is of His Son's Service

&

The Mother of a U.S. Soldier Named Leonard Cesternino Tells Her Son About a Dream She Had That They Were Together Again

&

In a Letter to His Dying Mother Back in the States, U.S. Army Chaplain Walter Hanley Thanks Her for Being Such a Good and Loving Parent

Two months before D-Day, Supreme Allied Commander Dwight D. Eisenhower wrote a private letter to his wife, Mamie, reflecting on the human cost of the war. "[I]t is a terribly sad business to total up the casualties each day," he wrote,

> *. . . [and recognize] that back home the news brings anguish and suffering to families all over the country. . . . War demands real toughness of fiber—not only in the soldiers that must endure, but in the homes that sacrifice their best.*

The sentiment is a timeless one, and troops serving in all conflicts recognize that their families in the States bear the brunt of war as intensely as anyone in uniform. But while the spouses, parents, and other relatives on the home front live in a constant state of anxiety, there is, intermingled with their apprehension, a profound sense of pride in their loved ones for serving their country. Gabriel C. Navarro, a first-generation immigrant from Mexico who was residing in Houston, Texas, articulated the feelings of many parents in the following letter to his son Porfirio, a twenty-two-year-old corporal in the Marine Corps. The letter was written on June 7, 1943, which marked the one-year anniversary of Porfirio's entry in the U.S. military.

ENVIO*.- A mi hijo PORFIRIO, en el primer ani-
versario de su ingreso al EJERCITO AMERICANO.

7 de junio de 1943..... fecha inolvidable
para todos nosotros.
7 de junio de 1943..... fecha gloriosa y
memorable para ti, hijo mio. Fecha que marco
una nueva etapa en tu existencia.
Un año hace hoy que, valiente y optimista
lleno de fe y amor patrio, te alejaste de nuestro lado, para ir a engrosar las filas del
Ejercito Americano; el Ejercito de las Demo-
cracias y de las Libertades. Doce meses de do-
lorosa ausencia, durante los cuales, nuestro
pensamiento y mi cariño paternal, han ido si-
guiendo tus huellas.
Te segui paso a paso a traves del Oceano
erizado de peligros, hasta llegar contigo a esa
tierra de valientes tan duramente castigada
por la metralla nipona.
Segui tus pasos hasta las intrincadas e
inhospitas selvas, y mi imaginacion te vio,
decidido y valiente, afrontando la muerte que
te rodeaba por doquier, para defender hasta
morir, tu bandera de las barras y las estre-
llas.
Noches de insomnio pasadas en la obscuri-
dad de mi alcoba, luchando contra el presenti-
mientosiniestro y cruel, de tu eterna separa-
cion, en las que mi corazon suspense su latir
al solo pensamiento de
sus alas sobre tu cabe
la Humanidad, me grita
nacion ante el pocible
siempre que este sacri
que si mas vidas, como
para nosotros, tuviera
to lo haria, en holocau
valor y entusiasmoque
nuestro lado para acud
tria que precisa la ay
hijos, me lleno de sat
ten la seguridad de qu

macita la que te diera el ser, te cubre
sus bendiciones y oraciones, como te cubri
Madre Patria con el lienzo sacrosanto de
bandera, que hoy ondea, inmensa y gloriosa
ese suelo que tu ayudaste a conquistar.
... ...
Hijo mio; haces falta en tu hogar. ...
el silencio y tristeza por tu ausencia. Hay
lo que en que nos parece escucharte voz vla-
momentos en que nos hace recordarte. Todo
ronil y llena, entonando canciones predilectas
tus pinturas, tus dibujos, tus libros y que
hoy yace todo quieto en el lugar donde tu los
dejaste al partir, parecen moverse impulsados
por manos invisibles, para hacer mas viva el
1 alma, la ilusion de tu presencia. Pero estas
ejos... inmensamente lejos de nosotros, sin
bargo, estas con nosotropues te llevamos en
stro pensamiento, en el corazon... Hijo mio
rido; si en los altos designios del Altisi-
sta, que seas tu entran la m... de tantos heroes que
diendo   campo de batalla,
           noble Ideal, quie-
           ire y para tu que-
           tanto, no moriras.
           razon; viviras
           cada objeto, ca-
           onserva incolume
                por que tu vi-
                nuestro lado,
                r el deber
                a libertad ga-
                os, de inmen-
                me importa-
                ros, oyendo-
                valor, y
                TORIA.

                    ro

243.

*Porfirio Navarro
(right), and the letter
by Gabriel Navarro
to his son*

It has been one year to the day that, courageous and optimistic, full of faith and love of country, you left our side to join the armed forces of America. The forces of Democracy and Liberty.

Twelve months of absence, during which time our thoughts and my paternal affection have followed you step by step across an ocean full of dangers. I arrived with you to that land which has been destroyed by the machine-guns of the Japanese. I followed your steps into the tangled and inhospitable jungles, and my imagination saw you, determined and valiant, defying death on all sides, and ready to defend until death your flag of stars and stripes. . . . My heart stops beating when I think of death extending its wings over your head. My great love of humanity cries to me for acceptance and resignation toward the possible sacrifice of your life, so long as this sacrifice is not in vain. . . .

The courage and enthusiasm which you demonstrated upon leaving us to answer your country's call, which needs the help of its children, filled me with satisfaction and pride. And you may be sure that your mother, who gave you life, also covers you with benedictions and prayers, just as your mother country covers you with its flag, which now waves immense and glorious upon that land which you are helping to conquer.

My son: You are missed in our home. There is a silence and a sadness because of your absence. Everything in the house reminds us of you. There are moments when it seems that we can hear your voice, singing your favorite songs. Your paintings, your sketches, your books, they all lie quietly where you left them upon your departure. They seem to move, impelled by invisible hands, to make more vivid, in my soul, the illusion of your presence. But you are far away . . . extremely far, from us, but yet, you are here with us, for we have you in our thoughts and in our hearts.

My dear son: If it is in the Almighty's great scheme of things, that you should be one of many heroes who meets death in battle, defending your flag and a noble ideal, I want you to know that to your father, as well as to your dear mother, who both love you very much, you will not die. You will still be alive in our minds and in our hearts. You will be living in our home, in which every object, every corner, every ray of light, will hold the memory of your presence.

But let's not talk of death, for you will live, my son, to return to our side, full of glory and satisfaction for having done your duty. You will return to enjoy a liberty won at a cost of bloody sacrifices and immense hardships, and then I will not care about anything except having you next to us, listening to you narrating your acts of heroism and bravery, and singing with you the hymn of Victory.

Gabriel C. Navarro

Like Navarro, whose son returned to him alive, the mother of Leonard Cesternino worried every day about her boy, and tried to focus on the joyful day when they would be together again. On December 1, 1943, Jennie Cesternino sent the following letter describing a dream of hers in which Leonard had finally come home and how elated she was to "see" him again. Unbeknownst to Mrs. Cesternino, Leonard had been killed in action in Italy on the very night, it is believed, his mother dreamed they were reunited. (Mrs. Cesternino was Italian herself, but she wrote the letter to her son in English, which was not her first language. Paragraph breaks have been added to make the letter easier to read.)

Dear Lenny,

Just writing to let you know we are all in good health hoping to hear the same from you. I didn't get any mail for this week yet but today is only Wenesday so I'll probaly have one by the end of this week

you know Son I'm feeling happy today

the reason is I dreamed about you last night and I saw you very plain in my dreams and that made me very happy

it was just like really seeing you

I dreamed you came in from work from Tony's and you came in all smiles and you said to me Ma you better send my pants to the cleaners because I have a date for tonight

it realy made me happy to see you even though it was only a dream and I hope and pray that this dream will come true and soon to see you come home from work and to be home for good this month will be Christmas and I hope God will be merciful and bring peace to the whole world

and even though we are far apart Son do try and have a merry Christmass and we will do the same but no matter how far apart we are we will be together in thought

I will be thinking of you every minuet of that day and will pray God to Bless and protect you till you come home safe back to me not that that's the only day I think and pray for you every day of course you know that but on that day it will be more so being that it's the first that you are away from home but I'm sure this war will be over soon and than we all will have something to be thankfull for so lets hope for the best O.K. Son don't forget to let me know how you spent Christmass day and remember we are all Lovingly thinking of you

Carmela and Sonny want me to say they Love you and Nicky hears them so he said so also

Love from all take good care of your self and God Bless you with all my Love

Mother

Just as parents like Mrs. Cesternino were anxious about their son (or daughter) serving in a war zone, troops on the front lines worried about their family members in the States. In the spring of 1944, thirty-nine-year-old Captain Walter Hanley, a Catholic chaplain serving with an evacuation hospital in New Guinea, learned that his mother back in Ohio was extremely ill and had little hope of recovery. Hanley urgently appealed to his superiors for a leave, but he knew that there was almost no chance he would make it to his mother's side before she died. The best he could do was write her a letter.

April 1, 1944

Dear Mama:

The Red Cross called me last night about the cablegram concerning your condition. I inquired immediately about the chances of getting home. The army will not give permission to return home under any condition other than the regular rotation of troops. About the only chance I have is to get on some list going home, and there is not much of a chance that that will be before August. I will do all I can & Fr. Gearhard is trying to help me.

You have been a good mother to us all, and all that we children have we owe to you. With Clarence's and Papa's deaths, your ill-health for years and the depression, your life has been a hard one—and yet your faith & your prayers have given you the strength to go on. When the train pulled out of the station I think you knew you would never see me again, and your strength has encouraged me all of these months. If God asks of you this sacrifice—for my work was needed here for these boys, I know you will have the strength to make it. The other priests here said their masses, as I did, this morning for you, and I know Almighty God will care for you.

You do not need to worry about us children. James is happily married and is a good husband and father. Kathleen will always have a home and James & I will see to it that she will be taken care of. Whatever good I may be able to do in the priesthood will be a testimony of your prayers and your struggles to bring me there.

I am thankful that you could have the good care of the sisters and St. Rita's and all that the hospital can give you. I know that Papa and Clarence are waiting for you and that our prayers will be for you every day until you join them in heaven. I know you will ever be a loving mother to Kathleen, James and his family and myself.

Your son, Walter

Chaplain Hanley was, in fact, granted a leave. He made it home two days before his mother passed away, and he was able to be with her in her final moments.

**Technical Sergeant Joe Graser Advises
His Younger Brother on What to Expect
as He Prepares for Basic Training**
&

**First Lieutenant Dave Albrecht Reminds
His Brother, an Infantryman Fighting in
Germany, That "God is a Powerful Help
[and Never] Forget to Call on Him!"**

*While some parents had only one child in the armed services to worry
about, many had several children in harm's way. After seeing their old-
est son, Joe, ship off to Europe with Patton's 3rd Army, William Graser
and his wife, Theresa, then watched as their youngest boy, Don, packed
up for basic training and left their home in New Richmond, Ohio. (Don
would later fight in the Pacific, and both boys, fortunately, would survive
the war.) The Grasers could take comfort in the fact that Joe was looking
after his younger brother and frequently offered him both military and
spiritual advice. Stationed in England at the time, twenty-three-year-old
Joe wrote his teenage brother on November 15, 1944, the following letter
instructing him on how to be a first-rate soldier—and a man of integrity.*

Dear Don:

I received word today that you took your physical, so if you are accepted by the
Army, I imagine you will have been inducted by the time you get this. At any rate,
I will presume that you are in or about to go. I have wanted to tell you a few things
about Army life. It is almost impossible to recite all the short cuts, all the rackets,
& all the little tricks, that can make things easier for you. No one can tell you these
things, they must all be learned, unfortunately, by experience, that sometimes are
very hard, & sometimes seems needlessly difficult.

There will be times, especially at first, that you will think you never saw such
bullheaded, roundabout, stupid men in your life. Many of these will be your superiors, & they will issue orders that contradict, cancel, reign you & your ideas

of success. You will live next to men, that represent types only known to you in the funny paper. Lots of these will have habits that are rare.

You may be tempted to tell yourself that you have been around enough to see a little of everything & everybody, but I'm telling you, you will be surprised to see some of them.

Remember this, the Army has a reason for everything it does, true, they attempt to doubt your intelligence to a certain degree, but only as a means of cooperation & teamwork.

Always think of that when things get pretty rough & you feel like sounding off. Blowing off steam to your superiors never got anybody anywhere here, or any place else. They have you sewed up backwards & front, & if you become too

Family photograph taken in the fall of 1942 when Joe Graser came home on leave from basic training (from left to right): Don (brother), Theresa (mother), Joe, William (father), Margaret Breller (sister), and Peggy Breller (niece)

loud, about what you consider your rights, you will be in for a big let down. Accept what they give you in the same spirit as if it were Mom or Dad telling you something to do.

This is about the men you will live with, and you will find that no matter how wrong any of them are, they all have real decent ideals in their hearts.

Try to understand & appreciate all their various ways of living. I will go as far as to say that even more than in the store or school, the more friends you can make, the better off you will be, as you discover when you finally get into the field, and are entirely depending upon those around you. You will be surprised at how often little friendships can benefit you. . . .

The Army will always take care of you in such things as food, clothing & medical care, but to make your living conditions more plesant, will be all up to you.

Be as kind and jolly as possible, for kindness & happiness will mean a lot to you, especially in your spare time.

Always remember, what ever your job may be, it is just as important in winning the war, as that of a General.

Something that keeps your mind off the tendency it will have toward complaining, & sweating out the things you see, is always keeping yourself in shape, & always looking ahead for methods of improving & making easy, the few hours you have to yourself. It is a true fact, that if you let yourself & equipment go down, your morale also goes with it. Take the time to keep it up to snuff, then you really can enjoy your spare time.

You will do your share of griping about the lousy conditions of this & that, but in the long run, griping will just get you down & makes you feel worse than it ever did.

As Mom always said you are judged by the company you keep, so don't be to hasty at first with whom you run around with, wait a while then pick out a buddy or so.

Another thing, always remember your a Catholic, you will see it's very easy to give your religion up, while in the service, since no one is there to remind you about it, but always live the way you were brought up, over two years ago when I came in Mom told me, to be careful & never to disgrace my name, that is something that has always been on my mind, in whatever I do, & surely has been a guidance to me.

At first your time will be very scarce, but never fail to drop the folks a line, even if its only a Hello, to let them know your OK, cause it is a terrible worry for both Mom & Dad when they don't hear from us.

Hope you don't take this as a Sunday sermon, I don't want it to impress you as such. You more than I perhaps have the facilities of hitting it off with anyone that comes along. Be at ease with everything, I know you will, never lose sight of the fact, no matter how bad things will get & they will, don't think they won't, that it is an honor to salute, stand retreat etc. A lot of guys will say your getting a raw deal, but these fellows can soon be recognized, & they just became a nuisantes.

I wish you a lot of luck Don, I regret deeply the necessity of you having to leave home & do this but it makes me mighty proud to have you as a partner on this team, & its not so bad in the long run, believe me.

Good Luck
Joe

At almost the same time that Technical Sergeant Joe Graser was in England, a twenty-three-year-old first lieutenant named Dave Albrecht was there, too, writing similar letters to his younger brother as well. While Dave was an officer in the Army Air Corps (predecessor to the U.S. Air Force), his brother Louie was a young private first class fighting in Germany. Dave was more concerned with his little brother's well-being than his own, and in the fall of 1944 he wrote Louie the following letter.

Dear Runt,

I don't know when I've been so glad to receive any letter as I was to receive yours of the 28th. It just got here today and I have been thinking you dead, crawling in snake infested jungles and many other unpleasant things. We in the Air Corps don't have to experience that kind of life. You told me on the 14th not to write until I got a new address from you but maybe this will get to you.

We just came back from a 48 hour pass. This time we went to Liverpool and Manchester. We rode the elevated train all along the docks and got a good look at some ocean going vessels. Then we rode the ferry from Liverpool to New Brighton and caught a Jeep for a ride through the tunnel back to Liverpool. The roof of the tunnel is just eighteen inches below the bed of the river and the river is probably seventy feet deep or better so you can imagine the pressure built upon the roof. I've forgotten my Physics enough so I can't figure it off hand.

We went to the stage play, "Junior Miss", in the evening and really got a laugh out of it. So far we have seen five plays while we have been here. I enjoy them more every time I go.

Last night was the party celebrating our 200th mission as a bomb group. It was quite a blow out with bands, liquor etc. But I came home early. I ate _five_ steaks for supper myself and felt much too contented to play around all evening. I had a total of one beer to drink and that was my evening.

But don't get the idea that life over here is just a bed of roses. We see enough of the rough stuff too. Our bombardier has been killed, all of our boys have been hit by flak except myself and the radio operator. Our tail gunner was shot down with another crew but is safe in a hospital in Belgium. I've seen planes go down in flames and crash where fighters hit our planes and the havoc they create is hard to believe. I've seen flak so heavy and thick you could actually land on the smoke puffs—yet we always manage to come through some way. I've seen planes come home so badly beaten up they could not fly for one month, yet the battle really isn't too bad. We don't think of past missions and we never look forward to a mission as anything more than another number to chalk up on our credit side. We do live a pretty jolly life, everything being considered and I have enjoyed most of it.

And believe me when I say that I, to whom religion meant not much of anything, receive the greatest comfort of all from knowing that the prayers of my wife and the folks are with me. God is a powerful help Runt: don't ever forget to call on him!

Patty is feeling fine and is getting more anxious every day for the arrival of our young one, I am anxious to know whether he will be a boy or girl.

Take good care of yourself Runt. Your Brother, Dave.

This was the last letter that Louie would receive from his brother; Dave Albrecht was gunned down only days later by enemy fire. Two months after Dave's death, Louie himself was shot in the head. Luckily, the bullet only grazed the top of his skull and he was sent back into combat after a three-month recuperation in the hospital. In February 1946, Louie returned to their home state of Nebraska and became a teacher. He was called up again for the Korean War and, after surviving that conflict as well, later became an administrative executive in the YMCA.

Chaplain George M. Phillips Writes to the Parents of a Fallen Hero and Assures Them That Their Son Never Lost His Faith in God
&
Chaplain H. E. Van Meter, Serving with the Marines in the Pacific, Writes Letters of Condolences to Two Parents Whose Sons Were Killed on Iwo Jima

For troops on the front lines, no letter is harder to write than a message of condolence to the loved one of a fellow soldier, Marine, airman, or sailor who has died. As they stare at that blank piece of paper in search of the right thing to say, they are well aware that every word they put down will be read carefully by a mourning parent, spouse, or some other family member in need of comfort. Drafting the letter can be all the more heartbreaking if the writer, himself, was close to the deceased. On April 30, 1945, almost one week before the war in Europe was over, a young

Army lieutenant named Donald Pound was killed when his platoon was pinned down by a German machine gun. Lieutenant Pound heroically directed the fire toward himself, allowing a second platoon to move into position and take out the machine gun nest. The regimental chaplain, Father George M. Phillips, had known the lieutenant well and sent the following letter to Pound's family.

Dear Mr. Pound:

You have undoubtedly already received word of the death of your son, 2ⁿᵈ Lieutenant Donald J. Pound, O-549401. He was killed in action on the 30ᵗʰ of April, 1945 in Czechoslovakia.

This is a very difficult letter for me to write because I knew Donald intimately. He introduced himself to me when I came into the Regiment, and he always was eager to help me in my work with the men. At Camp San Luis Obispo he served at a High Mass on the Feast of the Assumption. When the mission was held for the Division at Lompoc his assistance was invaluable. We came overseas on the same transport, and he served my Mass on board ship always receiving Holy Communion. Though days at the staging area were busy, he was conspicuously present at all services. Just a few days before his death I came to say Mass for his platoon. He assembled his men and served the Mass himself. In my experience there was no Catholic officer who ever practiced his faith more openly, and gave better example to his men in the reception of the sacraments, in attendance at Mass, and in the highest personal conduct than Lieutenant Pound. And the most striking part of it all his men admired him.

Although Donald's death was instant, I saw his body later and said a prayer for him. He was buried with full military honors by a Catholic Chaplain in a cemetery in Western Germany. I know there is little that I can say to take away your present grief except that you and Mrs. Pound worked and prayed through the years that your son would grow up to be a man of whom you could be proud in the eyes of God. You may be sure that you achieved that purpose in Donald. In this trial keep your faith in God, and see His good and gracious purpose working through it all.

May I express to you and Mrs. Pound my sincerest sympathy, and the promise of a continued remembrance of Donald in my Mass.

Sincerely yours,
George M. Phillips
Chaplain, 386th Infantry

Even if chaplains do not know a fallen hero, many of them still feel it is appropriate to send a word of sympathy to family members back in the States. Overwhelmed at times by the sheer volume of letters that must be written, some chaplains—understandably—use essentially the same language in each message. But many, like Herb E. Van Meter, tried to personalize as best they could every correspondence. Van Meter served as a chaplain with the Marine Corps' 5th Division in the Pacific, including when they stormed the island of Iwo Jima. Almost seven thousand Marines were killed during the fighting, and Van Meter wrote countless letters to the parents of the boys who did not survive. On April 2, 1945, he sent the following to Mrs. Linnie C. Buford in Portland, Oregon.

2 April 1945

My dear Mrs. Buford:

You have already learned through official channels of the death of your son, James Emory, in the action on Iwo Jima. There is nothing I can say or do to restore him to you, but perhaps it will comfort you to know that you are not alone in your grief, that we, his comrades, mourn him with you.

Marines are not inclined to show their feelings. The life is hard and they become hardened. But if you had seen with what tender care men decorated the graves of their buddies and if you had been with me as we left Iwo Jima you would know how hard it was to leave behind those who had fought beside me. As the transport left the anchorage the troops stood silently, reverently at attention in their honor. Eyes were fixed on the flag flying in the Division cemetery over their graves. It was a holy moment. Words cannot express the thoughts that rise in a man's heart at such a time. There were men thinking of James as there were men whose thoughts were with those who lie beside him under those white crosses. There were prayers and there were tears. We will not forget.

Time alone will heal the pain of separation from your son. Pride will help you face it now: pride in one who gave his life to his nation, pride in having given a gift so great. Faith will help: faith in those great causes for which Jim risked and gave his life, faith in the dedication of our people and nation to those causes. And most of all there is faith in Almighty God to help you, faith in Him who gives us life and in whose providence it is taken from us.

God grant you that faith.

Faithfully yours,
Chaplain, USNR
H.E. Van Meter

Van Meter regularly put himself in danger to minister to his men during operations in the Pacific, and he made it home alive in 1945.

Ruth Kwall Assures Her Fiancé, Joseph Portnoy, That, No Matter How Long the War Lasts, "I'll Wait for You Forever"
&
In a Short but Poetic Letter to Ruth, Staff Sergeant Portnoy Affirms Both His Faith in God and His Undying Love for Her
&
Staff Sergeant Portnoy Writes to Ruth About a Yom Kippur Service on the Front Lines That Was Particularly Meaningful to Him

"My Angel," Ruth Kwall began a letter to her fiancé, Joseph Portnoy, the day after the Japanese struck Pearl Harbor. Kwall and Portnoy, a true patriot

who was the son of a Russian immigrant and had joined the Army a year before the December 7, 1941, attack, both realized that he would soon be off to war. "You know, dear, for some reason or other I took particular notice of 'my' ring today," Kwall went on to write:

It shined more brightly than ever before—in this dark day a beacon of hope. It seemed to want to talk—to tell me that just as it is without end, but continues on in an unbroken line, so our love is without end. For instance—I want to tell you again, more surely than ever, that no matter how long or hard the siege may be I'll wait for you forever.

I know, and darling you must too, that God in heaven will guard this precious thing and help preserve it and us for a time when the world will need tangible examples to show it that war does not end things; that good, beautiful emotions live on forever. I'm nineteen, Joe, but I know deep down inside me that the emotion I feel, <u>that we feel</u>, is older, is mature—that it has made me grow to more of the sort of person you'd have me be.

Ruth Kwall and Joseph Portnoy

War isn't funny and I know we'll be tested even further than we ever dreamed could be possible. I'm game, honey. I love you. I'm going to bed now, sweet, and of course I'll dream of you.

Need I say I'm yours,
Ruthy

Portnoy was sent to Fort Meade for more training, and it wasn't until December 1943 that, after he was granted a three-day pass, he and Ruth were married. By the end of June 1944, Staff Sergeant Portnoy and the rest of his battalion (967th Field Artillery) were stepping on European soil to begin the massive Allied invasion into France and Germany. Portnoy was extremely limited in what he could report, but he frequently wrote about his faith, which, like his love for Ruth, never faltered.

August 11, 1944

My dearest own:

Yes angel, you are wise to rely on your complete faith that everything will turn out right for us, and knowing that you think like that, I also feel free to exercise my faith. Perhaps some may feel that we are vain and view the eventualities of war through rose-colored glasses, but if that were so, then how could we believe in prayer and that a world of peace is possible? No, sweet, as long as we can believe that our lives are still molded by God's will, and believe in his justice, we can never be accused of deliberately sugarcoating our senses.

It's so odd the way the meaning of love continually seems to turn corners, and around each corner we view a broader, more beautiful horizon. With you beside me, courage becomes a living thing, and there will be little that we can't surmount. Of course we're idealistic kids with our heads tilted skyward, but that's just the way we are heading. It's just right over that dark cloud, honey. Can't you see that sun?

Your adoring husband

Despite his optimism, Portnoy was not unaware of the terrible cost of war, and on September 27, 1944, he wrote the following letter about the customs and traditions that helped him and his men stay resilient during trying times. (Ruth had also just given birth to a healthy boy—their first child—whom they named Bobby.)

My dearest own:

Today continued with its uneventfulness, and though it's remained disturbing, it did give us the opportunity of celebrating Yom Kippur properly. We had a service that lasted all morning and it was quite inspiring. I especially took note of the Yizkor service. Death over here has become such a light matter that I'd almost forgotten that it was accompanied by sadness. But at the service, the rabbi again gave us the theme of the old attitude of returning to God and everlasting life. It sunk deeply and made me realize that the toughness of war can easily be erased once we return home, to our churches and synagogues again, and begin building the stones of civilization over the callous savagery that we find in war. There will be a successful returning, don't fear darling.

Ruth and Bobby Portnoy

Were you well enough to attend the briss, darling? I can imagine how much joy the family received from that. We haven't had one in ages. I seem to miss the best things, don't I? It won't be long though. My days away will be amply repaid, even by having a smile from your eyes. The lost years will seem as a day compared to the joy that I'll have when I hold my son in one arm and have the other securely turned about you. You just erase all of my troubles, just by being with me. Gosh, how I adore you. I can tell you that over and over again, and each time I mean it with a new freshness of emotion. It's marvelous to have a love that's always in its springtime. Tickle Bobby's feet for me.

Your's ever, Joe

Portnoy returned to the States and was honorably discharged from the Army in June 1945.

Lieutenant Sydney H. Brisker Describes to His Parents How He and His Fellow Sailors Held a Passover Seder Aboard the USS *Beaumont*

Although he could have been medically deferred due to a torn cartilage in his right knee, Sydney H. Brisker did not reveal his condition to the military so that he could join the Navy and fight for his country. Brisker, a twenty-eight-year-old architect originally from Bethlehem, Pennsylvania, would ultimately serve for more than three and a half years and live through six major battles and four invasions. Along with being extremely patriotic, he was a deeply religious man, and he made every effort to practice his faith no matter where he was or what he was doing at the time. This was often a challenge—but, as the following letter about a Seder he celebrated aboard the USS Beaumont *indicates, not impossible.*

Dear Mother and Dad,

The ghosts of thousands of years of Jews were with me tonight—from the first refugees of the Bible's fascist Pharaoh through two destructions of the Temple and through ages of wandering and persecution—they were with me tonight at the strangest Seder I've ever had.

In the jungle heat of Guadalcanal and the torridness of the African desert, in the biting cold of Iceland and Alaska, and the foggy dampness of England, modern Maccabeans in the uniforms of their beloved countries gathered tonight to celebrate the deliverance of the Jews from the persecution of an ancient Fascism. The modern parallel is quite startling at first. It can be said, without fear of contradiction, there are no Jews in the ranks of the enemy.

When I look back upon all the Seders I've sat at, in my own home with my beloved family, and in strange cities with friends, I wonder if I could have ever dreamed that I might be spending a Passover on a U.S. warship, bound on a mission of war. Or perhaps, I should say, a mission of peace, because we are fighting for the peace for which each Passover we lift our voices in prayer.

One enlisted man (ship's cook, third class) and myself are the only Jews aboard the Beaumont, but we decided to spend the Passover with a Seder. At our last port of call we obtained two boxes of matzoh, and a hagadah from the Chaplain. Alcoholic beverages are prohibited aboard U.S. men-of-war, and grape juice was unobtainable, so we substituted prune juice for wine. The Captain said he would cooperate in every way possible to help us hold our Seder.

We got two chickens from the chief commissary steward. (I am the commissary officer, a recent appointment, so it was easily arranged). For bitter herb we used stalks of Chinese cabbage; and for parsley we used the celery tops. The officer's steward baked a sponge cake. Everything else was quite orthodox—to the salt water and hard-boiled egg. But lacking matzoh-meal, there were no knadels. That would have been something to see—the matzoh balls rolling around with the motion of the ship.

A bay in the Chief Petty Officer's quarters was partitioned off by hanging two blankets, and the Seder was set at a table large enough for eight. We had several guests, the pharmacist's mate 1/c, a Protestant, another ship's cook, who is Catholic, and two Steward's mates who are colored Baptists, as well as the officer's steward. And to this gathering I related the story of Passover in English in answer to the Four Questions as asked by Goldstein.

The modern parallel was more startling. When I read "And it is this same promise which has been the support of our ancestors and of us too: for at every time enemies rise against us, to annihilate us; but the most Holy, blessed be He, hath delivered us out of their hands" I could substitute Hitler for the Assyrian Laban who intended to kill every Jew—root out the whole race.

And I read a prayer, which has been repeated for centuries, and today more loudly than ever "May He who maketh peace in His heavens grant peace on us and all Israel, and say ye, Amen."

But if I was startled by the modern parallelism, it was the myriad of ghosts of long dead Jews, visiting me tonight, who make me feel that this prayer for peace need not be repeated year in and year out. We have the answer in our power now. The United Nations can make this Victory one of everlasting Peace and build a world in which Jew and Gentile, white and colored, live in peace, harmony and security—just like we of different faiths and races sat down at Seder tonight.

Good night, dear parents—God Bless You.

All my love, Syd.

⚔️ **Ensign Charles Edward Sweeney Writes to His Cousin Esther Back in the States About a Christmas Day He Will Never Forget**
&
Lieutenant Edward L. Pulaski Sends His Sweetheart, Sara "Mickey" Rooney, a Very Special Christmas Message

For servicemen and women thousands of miles from their loved ones in any war, holidays often prompt mixed emotions. Thoughts of friends and family members gathered together provide them with fond memories to help pass the time and, most important, give them something for which to hope. But it also makes them all the more homesick. While stationed aboard a subchaser anchored near the hot, tropical islands of the Philippines in December 1944, a twenty-three-year-old ensign from Rhode Island named Charles Edward Sweeney was trying to enjoy the spirit of the season as much as possible. In a letter written to a favorite cousin on Christmas Day, Sweeney explained that a sudden turn of events caused him to forget about all that he was missing and appreciate, instead, the most precious gift of all—life itself.

Dear Esther,

All morning the turkeys roasted in the oven; the cook was busy with all the fixings which we'd managed to beg, borrow or steal from other ships or from nearby Army quartermasters.

With the exception of the cook and his helpers, there wasn't much work for the rest of us to do. We were lying to in a little inlet which is described in dispatches as an "advanced base." When we first arrived here, all hands were excitedly talking of the Japanese and of air raids and of possible hand-to-hand encounters with other enemy small craft. . . .

The war was so near and yet so far away. This was Christmas and there was a handsome dinner to enjoy. Nothing loomed to mar it; our minds were free because the ship had, ever since it's launching, patrolled far-off and friendly waters and our imaginations were not yet colored by the real tinge of war.

It was nearly noon and time for dinner when another camouflaged ship entered the inlet, signaled us by blinker for permission to tie up alongside us, and then made a quick berth with both screws turning full. Most of us were lolling around the deck and paid little attention to the routine mooring of the other ship until it was firmly secured to our side and one of its hatches was opened and a stretcher passed topsides by two sailors who handled their burden with great care.

The soldier on the stretcher had his arm and part of his shoulder torn off. His

Charles Sweeney with his mother and sisters

unconscious form was limp on the canvass; his fatigue suit was torn and bloody, his young features were frozen into hard lines.

The stretcher was passed over onto our deck, carried across to the other ship and then onto the beach where there was a waiting truck, in a small dirt road which led off into the brush and to a forward evacuation hospital. As the stretcher was placed in the truck, a large white tag bearing the soldier's name, outfit, and a description of his wounds, became undone and fluttered to the road. Someone picked it up and tied it again around his ankle.

The second stretcher passed up the hatch was completely covered by a blanket, and so was the third.

Next we saw a sailor aboard the other ship reach down the hatch and help another soldier mount the ladder. He wore the familiar fatigue clothes, bowl-shaped tin helmet, and heavy boots which were unlaced. One foot followed the other mechanically. Someone helped him over the gangway to our ship and as he walked past us one of the assisting sailors said "shell shock" and we noticed the vacant look in the soldiers eyes which seemed widened by a recent horror. The man got across the inboard ship to the beach with assistance across the gangways.

Several others like him passed now. It was hard to read their ages; some looked as though they were fifty years old at nineteen; others looked as though they had been born as old men. All wore tin hats and the jungle fatigues; all clutched their rifles as they walked.

The last soldier to pass was bareheaded and he had his arms around the shoulders of the two sailors who had locked their arms under him to make a seat. The soldier's trousers were rolled up to the knees—just above where the bandages which were rolled down to and over his feet started. The last soldier seemed the youngest of them all and merely stared straight ahead as he was carried by.

We watched in complete silence while the small Army truck drove off carrying the three stretcher cases and the soldier with the wounded legs.

The "walking wounded" stood idly by on the beach. All still carried their rifles firmly. Only one sat down, exhausted. . . . Nobody spoke for about a minute and then there were numerous questions asked of the sailors aboard the newly arrived ship. Yes, one of them said, the wounded had been in action "up there" and we all followed the sailors eyes up the coastline where a long peninsula jutted into the sea.

Last night this bunch had caught hell, he said, and added something about a detachment being cut off and almost entirely wiped out. The ship had taken what was left of them off the beach after a sector had been regained.

Then the talking on deck stopped. The sailors on the other two ships all went below for Christmas chow. In a few minutes, our own cook stuck his head out of

The subchaser on which Sweeney wrote his Christmas letter

the galley hatchway and called "chow's down." He seemed surprised when there was no rush for choice seats at the table. He was surprised until somebody talked to him. And then we all ate a handsome and delicious dinner together, in the crew's quarters, officers and men, in almost complete silence.

That's it Esther. It happened about two hours ago and it's affected me very powerfully. My fingers actually feel leaden as I type. Yet, I feel so heavily somber that I feel I have to tell somebody and you've always been a good listener.

We've been near enough to see things like this for quite a while. But for some reason or other, hand of God I guess, we've been completely immune. It wasn't much that I saw either. It was just a little side issue, just a pebble in a sea of trouble, and all we saw were the immediate afteraffects. So, this is Christmas, and it's the saddest one I've ever known. I wish you'd keep this letter to yourself, at least, <u>completely away from the rest of the family</u> . . . .

Life gave me a Christmas present a couple of hours ago; it's a gnawing appreciation of what all this means to all the people, usually the little and insignificant people, who have to go through agony. The war was personalized for me a couple of hours ago in the faces and battered figures of a handful of ruined men.

I'm sorry this had to be such a sad letter. But I just want to tell somebody and when I have something like this to tell I want to tell it to somebody close to me and who thinks and feels a lot like I do. And you've always been the closest that way.

We'll probably be moving out of here after a while. Then I'll try a cheerful and funny epistle about the heat and the bugs and the natives and how the movie cameras splutter aboard the big ships at places farther away. Until then, lots of love, Esther, and write as soon as you can.

Charlie

Like Charles Sweeney, twenty-five-year-old Edward L. Pulaski, a lieutenant in the Army Air Corps fighting overseas in 1944, also found himself in a reflective mood as the holidays approached. Pulaski was flying B-29s in the CBI (China-Burma-India) theater, and he had witnessed his share of death and destruction. But whenever his spirits started to sag, all he had to do was think of the beautiful young woman waiting for him back in Salina, Kansas, twenty-one-year-old Sara "Mickey" Rooney. The two had been introduced by a mutual friend and fell in love almost immediately. After dating for only a few months, Pulaski was mobilized and the two were separated. In late November 1944, he sent Rooney the following letter so that it would come before Christmas. And he had arranged, through a friend, for her to receive a special gift at the same time that the letter arrived.

My dearest Mickey,

Somehow I've got to put Christmas spirit into this letter while in a country that seldom sees snow except atop it's tallest northern mountains. Somehow I've got to pass on the spirit of good will towards men when all around me and myself are so sick and tired of being away that there is little good will even among us. Some-

November 25, 1944

My dearest Mickey,

Somehow I've got to put Christmas spirit into this letter while in a country that seldom sees snow except atop it's tallest northern mountains. Somehow I've got to pass on the spirit of good will towards men when all around me and myself are so sick and tired of being away that there is little good will even among us. Somehow I've got to say "Peace on Earth" when perhaps tomorrow I'll kill thousands of people. Somehow I've got to present you with both a gift and a token that means we are very close to each other though we couldn't be farther apart on this earth than we are right now.

Yet it is very easy for me to picture the snow that I've always seen at Christmas, feel the good will towards men that down deep all of us here try to feel above it all, honestly say "Peace on Earth" along with hun-

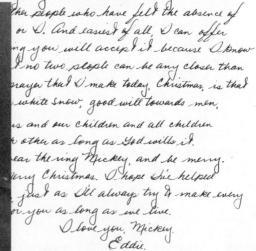

ther people who have felt the absence of ... or I. And easiest of all, I can offer ...ng you will accept it because I know ...t no two people can be any closer than ...rayer that I make today, Christmas, is that ... white snow, good will towards men, ...s and our children and all children ...r other as long as God wills it. ...ear the ring Mickey, and be merry. ...erry Christmas. I hope I've helped ... just as I'll always try to make every ...or you as long as we live.

I love you, Mickey.
Eddie.

Edward Pulaski, and his letter

how I've got to say "Peace on Earth" when perhaps tomorrow I'll kill thousands of people. Somehow I've got to present you with both a gift and a token that means we are very close to each other though we couldn't be farther apart on this earth than we are right now.

Yet it is very easy for me to picture the snow that I've always seen at Christmas, feel the good will towards men that down deep all of us here try to feel above it all, honestly say "Peace on Earth" along with hundreds of millions of other people who have felt the absence of peace more than you or I. And easiest of all, I can offer you this ring knowing you will accept it because I know you feel as I,—that no two people can be any closer than you or I. And the prayer that I make today, Christmas, is that we'll always have our white snow, good will towards men, peace on earth for us and our children and all children forever after, and each other as long as God wills it.

Edward and Sara Pulaski in 1996

So wear the ring Mickey, and be merry. For me this is a Merry Christmas. I hope I've helped make yours the same, just as I'll always try to make every single day happy for you as long as we live. I love you, Mickey.

Eddie

Edward Pulaski came home from the war in March 1945, and two weeks after returning he and Rooney got married. They raised four children and remained together for fifty-eight years, until, in 2002, Pulaski passed away.

After Several Candid Conversations with Fellow Troops About Infidelity, First Lieutenant Roy Fisher Tells His Wife How Proud He Is of Their Love for and Commitment to One Another

Separated for months and even years during the war, most couples found the time away from one another to be unbearable. Some became unfaithful, while others worked hard to honor the vow they had made to their loved one, no matter how difficult being apart may have felt. Only three months after getting married, First Lieutenant Roy "Jack" Fisher had to say good-bye to his wife, Joyce, when he deployed to Europe to fly B-17s over Germany. Fisher was madly in love with Joyce and wrote to her as often as he could. In March 1945, he sent the following letter to emphasize how pleased he was with their relationship and the high moral standards to which they strived to adhere.

Sunday nite March 11—

Joyce Darling,

I haven't written for two nites cause I ran out of stamps and I know you won't get these till I get home anyway. But I miss these nitely chats so much that I'm gonna write you anyway and just save the letters till I get home & then if you want to read them then—I'm sweating out orders now. My two room mates got on orders today and I got here when they did so it shouldn't be too long now.

I had quite an interesting day today darling. It all started out by my going to chapel like a good boy. Tex went with me and when we got started back to the barracks we got to cussing & discussing the sermon. He had said that the time had come for us to place our faith in God rather than in physical tangeable things. We should love our neighbors and look toward Christ and his teachings to help us in the peace that follows this war. We should get out of the rocking boat and walk on the water. Of course that isn't possible without tremendous faith and so he really had a point. Well we got started on the love your neighbor idea and we really had it out.

Then we went to see This is the Army this afternoon and while we were waiting for the show to start we got to talking to a fellow who had just come back from Sweden. He got to talking about the girls over there and the kind of deal they had. He said that he got a girl to keep house and cook his meals & so on. It seems that they take a very liberal view on couples living together—sort of trial marriage idea—. Well—when we got back to the sack we got on the subject of sex, fidelity and how different it is over here in these older countries than it is at home. Then of course that brought up the old argument about the double standard. How the wife should be a virgin regardless but that it really makes no difference as far as the man is concerned. Well—darling—you know I don't believe that and I know you don't. At any rate it was quite a discussion.

But to get back to the show. Remember the scene where the girl finally prevailed upon him to get married and they were joined by an army chaplain in the wings of the theater. I closed my eyes when they started saying the vows and I saw the prettiest bride in the world. Dressed in a white linen suit she stood there beside me as the service went along and then she turned to me and looked me straight in the eye and said she'd be mine forever. I could look right into your heart that day my darling. I could read your heart more clearly than I ever did before and I knew that you meant it with all your heart and soul and I hoped that you could read my heart too. I wanted you to know that my heart and soul reflected & radiated the same truth & sincerity which yours revealed to me. Yes—darling—I cried this afternoon tears of joy filled my eyes as I remembered that kiss that made you my wife forever. And then I wanted you beside me more than anything else in the world. I wanted to have your hand in mine so we could repeat those vows to each other and reaffirm them in each others hearts & souls. And I wanted to hold you in my arms darling and feel your breast pressed close to mine.

Dearest—I want you so very much. Because I love you so very muchly—

Nite sweetheart
Jack

Fisher returned to the arms of his wife four weeks later. They raised seven daughters (their only son died of cancer) and remained happily married.

Only Days After Being Liberated from a German POW Camp, Private First Class James F. Norton Writes a Jubilant Letter to His Parents Proclaiming "By the Grace of My Lord and Savior I Am Here Today"

"Dearest Mom and Dad," Private First Class James F. Norton began a letter to his parents back in St. Paul, Minnesota, on April 15, 1945. "This is the second happiest moment of my life," the nineteen-year-old soldier continued,

> *at last a chance to write home. The happiest moment came a few days ago when the greatest army in the world liberated me. Things have been happening so fast to me since I've been liberated, my head is still spinning. As much as I've cussed the army, I love it now, and I've never seen a more smooth working, efficient organization.*

Norton especially wanted his parents to know that the experience of being wounded and captured, as terrible as it had been, had one positive effect—it had made him a more religious man. He went on to write:

Gosh, there's so much to say, I don't even know how to start, and to tell the truth I don't know what I'm allowed to write or not.

I'm back in a huge, beautiful hospital in France, so I guess it won't be very hard for you to guess where I am. I've received nothing but the greatest of kindness from every one, and I never could put it in words what it feels like to be treated as a human being again. I am so happy I don't know whether to laugh or cry. Today we had the meal I've been dreaming about for 4 months - steak and french fries, and how--how I've been eating.

I'll never forget as long as I live when I saw that first Yank. I always said I'd kiss the first one I saw who liberated us, even if it were a 2nd Looie, and you guessed it, he was. He was more surprised than I, and I imagine it's the first time in history an officer has ever been kissed by an enlisted man. Then they gave us chocolate bars and cigarettes and I went wild. From there to here it has been a smooth job of evacuation.

I was shot and taken prisoner on the memorable day - Dec. 16, the first day of the terrific German breakthrough in the Ardennes, when all hell broke loose. The next four months I will tell about when I get home, and will describe them now in two words, Living Hell.

My leg is just about well now, and I'm here more or less to be built up. It will only be a short stay and I should be back in the States soon, Mom, and when I do get home, I'll probably never get farther than the back porch, as I've had all the excitement and adventure to last me a lifetime.

This is a small world. I never saw Bob Muyre from the day I got captured until now, and I often wondered what happened to him, and here we run into each other in the same ward of the huge hospital, and we both came in the same day. He was also shot in the leg but went to a different place and was also liberated a few days ago. Gosh, were we happy to see each other. Now my biggest concern is what happened to Red Deal, the best friend I ever had, and a lot of my other buddies. There's a million things I want to learn now that I'm back in contact again.

My biggest concern and something that has always been on my mind is how you two are and how the Missing in Action affected you. But you are both brave, strong parents so I'm sure everything is all right.

We were all saddened very much yesterday by the death of our great leader and a real buddy to every G.I. Joe, President Roosevelt. But it was God's will, and I hope that President Truman can fill his shoes.

Death has faced me many times in the past months and by the grace of my Lord and Savior I am here today to write this letter. I always considered myself a good Christian until I was captured, and then I learned what a fool I had been and what it really means to have faith and the power of prayer. I prayed day and nite, and these prayers were heard with the result that today I can really call myself a good Catholic and firm believer in the will of God.

I could fill up pages, but there's so much I'd rather tell than write, and so much more I want to know about you, Johnny and Bill. This is a poor attempt for my first letter, but I find it much more difficult than I expected. I hope to be in the States before I get an answer. To see your faces again will be the happiest moment of my life. I love you both and thank God every day I have such wonderful parents.

Your loving son, Jim

The Korean War

En Route to Korea, Captain Molton A. Shuler Jr. Laments to His Family That He Misses Them Already

&

Shuler Writes Home About an Improvised Church Service That He and Fellow Soldiers Celebrated in the Midst of Battle

A veteran of World War II, twenty-nine-year-old Captain Molt Shuler was attending the University of South Carolina Law School in Columbia when his reserve unit was called back to active duty after the communist North Korean army invaded South Korea in June 1950. As a student, married man, and father, Shuler could easily have obtained a deferment, but he felt an obligation to serve his country once again. While en route to Asia (via Alaska), he wrote the following letter to his wife, Helen, and began with a brief message to their four-year-old son, Duane. ("Sissy" is their daughter, Sheryl, who was not yet two.)

8 May 1952

My Dear Little "Bubba"—

Tomorrow you will be four years old—but when this letter reaches you your birthday will be past. Daddy wishes he could have been with you to help you celebrate—maybe next year when you are five Daddy will be there. Anyway, I

Molton and Helen Shuler

hope your present came in time. And I hope you will enjoy looking at your books and having Mommie read them to you. . . .

While Daddy is away I want you to eat all of your big man food so you'll be ready to fish with Daddy when he gets home. And I want you and "Sissy" to do just what Mommie says for you to do 'cause you have to take care of Mommie now that Daddy is away. Will you promise to be a good boy? I know you will.

Daddy will write again later—when he gets to Japan. God bless you and "Sissy."

Daddy loves you so much.

Daddy

P.S. You must give this page of your letter to Mommie for her to read—o.k.? That's a good boy.

My dearest—words won't describe the hurt in my heart to be moving further away from the one and only perfect wife on earth with each tick of the clock. I feel all choked up and my heart seems as if it is being torn out of my body. In fact I don't really have a heart anymore—I left it with you. For where you are is my whole life. Only the times when I receive mail from you will it be again in my body—for your words and thoughts will be you for the minutes I have to read and think of you. At times it may be hard for you to love me—but try hard, won't you? No effort on my part to love you is necessary—for you are easy—so easy to love.

I'll mail this in Anchorage—but I shan't write again until I am in Japan—for I want to do some reading in a Field Manual.

All my love—for always
Molt

Just over two weeks later, Shuler was in Korea. But despite the harsh conditions and stress of combat, he nevertheless found himself in an up-beat mood. Hunkered down in Chorwon, just north of the 38th Parallel, he sent the following letter.

Sunday nite 25 May 1952

Helen my Darling—

You are perfection—the paragon of womankind—and you're my wife—and I adore you! And what's more, your first 6 letters came today! With them came my very life—for my heart was slowly breaking for words of love and tenderness from you, my beloved wife. It's impossible to describe what your letters meant to me. More than you can possibly imagine I appreciate your love. I know full well you love me—but I can't see quite why. But I'm not going to quibble. I'm only going to love you more for loving me as you do.

Then there is another reason for my good spirits tonite—as if your letters were not enough. I went to church tonite. Let me paint you a word picture of the "church". Picture a grassy hillside surrounded by mountains. And a rugged looking—crew hair cut and all—chaplain dressed in fatigues standing by a Government Issue folding podium with a red velvet cover and brass candelabra minus candles, all placed on a couple of ammo boxes.

Then just left of the "pulpit" as you face it you find a battered, 30-odd key, olive drab organ, a GI pianist seated on a 5 gallon gasoline can. And in the background you find blasted Chinese bunkers and old gun emplacements. Then if you look way to your left you'll see a battery of 6 105 howitzers, their ugly muzzles pointed menacingly toward the North. To the right and on up the valley are bunkers of our company, a couple of tents from which winds a road (one way) behind our "church".

But what about pews and who occupys them? Well, they are roughly terraced rows with a handful of soldiers, mostly a little dirty and bedraggled, trying to keep from becoming more soiled by sitting on their helmets. You find a rifle loaded with a full clip, or a carbine with a jam-packed magazine beside each man. Over there is a blond and baby faced young man, and beside him is a tough looking hombre with a dark beard and dirty fingernails. And down in the front row are

Duane and Sheryl Shuler

three Korean boys who just sang a couple of hymns in their native tongue, self-conscious to be sure, but, even so, attesting to God's presence in the hearts of a people torn by war.

And God is in this "chapel"—so near you can almost reach out and touch him.

And the chaplain says, "And men, in the days to come, you must remember the words of Christ when asked where He lived; 'come and see' ".

Only a couple of times in my life before this evening, have I felt God's presence in such a way. Perhaps it was the place and the time—I don't know. Be that as it may, I liked the way I felt.

'Scuse me for trying to be literary. I didn't mean to—as my efforts no doubt reveal.

Goodnite dear and love our children for me—and miss me, please.

Your man always—
Molt

"By now you have no doubt been notified that I was scratched up a bit on the morning of the 16th," Shuler wrote to his wife on June 18. He had been struck in the neck, back, and leg by shrapnel and was quickly rushed to a MASH unit. He was then sent to the Tokyo Army Hospital to be treated for his wounds. From Japan he wrote:

> *I expect to have everything recleaned and stitched sometime this afternoon or tonight. It will be several weeks—perhaps four—before I leave here. . . . Don't tell people I'm hurt bad—I'm not—and it's no use to make a mountain out of a mole hill.*

His injuries, in fact, were not life-threatening. But in a tragic turn of events, Shuler is believed to have received infected blood plasma during his treatment, and, while still in Japan, he died of hepatitis on August 24, 1952.

◦═◦ The Vietnam War ◦═◦

◦═◦ **Chaplain Ray W. Stubbe Offers Reverend
Charles E. Witt His First Impressions of the
Marine Base at Khe Sanh, Vietnam**
　&
**In a Letter to Friends Back Home, Stubbe
Marvels That in Spite of the "Despicable"
Living Conditions, He Sees Examples of Faith
All Around Him**
　&
**On the First Day of What Would Be a Lengthy
Siege of Khe Sanh, Stubbe Assures His Parents
That He Is Still Alive**

*"I feel this is where I should be," Lieutenant Ray W. Stubbe, a Lutheran
chaplain serving with the 1st Battalion, 26th Marines, wrote from Vietnam to a fellow minister back in the States. "The Spirit has been working in me here," Stubbe continued in his letter, dated August 16,
1967—one day after his twenty-ninth birthday.*

> *From early in the morning to late at night, often through excruci-
> atingly arduous patrols, often in fear of paralyzing situations,
> through personal privations, through sights that cause tears, we
> continue in the labor of Our Lord, bringing the confidence of His*

*concern for all persons individually, His strength-giving Presence
amidst all the difficulties of our path.*

*Military chaplains like Stubbe have risked their lives in every American
conflict since the War of Independence, and many have been killed in the
line of duty. When Stubbe left his home in Milwaukee in the summer of
1967 to serve in Vietnam, he knew that the dangers were significant. But,
as he expressed in the following letter to Reverend Charles E. Witt, the
pastor of his church in Wisconsin, he believed that he was obliged to go
where God had called him.*

Evangelical Lutheran Church of the Redeemer

1933 West Wisconsin Avenue

Milwaukee, Wisconsin 53233

Dear Pastor Witt (and others in the upper room):

Please excuse not having written earlier, but I have been in a somewhat unsettled situation, and have finally been given a permanent "roost" here in Khe Sanh, in the extreme upper north and west area of Viet Nam. At least here it is perhaps the coolest area in Viet Nam, although it is very rainy and the monsoons will be upon us very soon. We are surrounded by mountains and everything is very beautiful. Many of the men here remark how this area could be one of the most beautiful areas in the world for a vacation—but the war situation. We, of course, live in bunkers, mainly underground, all of which involves living with the infected rats. One rat recently was on my feet! I woke up at about 4, stretched my legs out, and heard a barrage of squeaks—all I could think of were the 12 rabbies shots in my stomach! The catholic chaplain had one fall right on his bare chest!

The people here are tops. They are courteous, kind, considerate, one to another. They work very hard, often in the most unfavorable of circumstances, yet do it willingly. The Christians that are here are so openly and provide a tremendous witness to others. Many read their Bibles daily, lead a meaningful prayer life. I have huge attendances at my worship services—often perhaps ALL the protestants attached. I have had offerings also—and I don't receive 5¢ of military currency, but often receive $1.00 bills, sometimes a $5.00 bill! I conduct about one worship service each day, and four on Sundays—so you can see I am very busy. I hop from one hill to another (each hill is occupied by a company), stay over night in their war situation, conduct a service, talk with the men, and leave for the next hill. This has involved dozens of helocopter flights over hostile areas. We have the most trying counselling cases—men paralyzed with fear, anxiety; problems concerning those back home. The need is indeed very great!

Ray Stubbe at 4 months, 10 days. The photograph was taken on Christmas Day 1938 and shows that Stubbe was "prayerful" even as a toddler.

Things are fairly quiet here right now. The base hasn't been attacked since late June. We are surrounded by thousands of enemy—North Vietnamese troops, and can perhaps expect a massive attack in the next month or so—so please remember us in your prayers!—we certainly need them!

Faithfully,
Ray Stubbe

Several months later, Stubbe updated two friends from home about how he and his men were faring at Khe Sanh. Not surprisingly, there were moments of both joy and sorrow.

25 November 1967

Dear Ellen and Jim:

Thank you so much for the thoughtful letter and the first seasons card which I have received. I am not able to reciprocate with a card since we have none of those luxuries here where I am, so a letter will have to suffice.

It is good to hear that Bob Louis was ordained—but Texas?! Should you happen to have his address, I'd like to drop a letter to him, but, of course, from past experience, I probably cannot expect to receive a reply. It was also good to hear you were able to be back in Waukesha and renew old acquaintances. But most of all, it was good to hear that your thesis is completed and that you would probably be defending it this month. I am anxiously awaiting to hear the results.

It must be very gratifying to work with young minds which are still in the process of forming world views, or, should I say, giving intellectual formulations to some views of life, especially in the area of ethics. . . .

It is impossible not to impose a value system on other people, because we all live together in a society. My value of living in a filthy manner, or free love, of non support to activities beyond my purview, all have social implications—spreading

Chaplain Stubbe, far right, with U.S. Marines on Christmas Day 1968

of disease, increase in social disease, the remaining growth of evil. Not to decide to help the brother in need is itself a decision.

I am convinced as I have never been convinced before that the Gospel is the only solution—that is, when people are more concerned with giving than getting, with self-giving than self-fulfillment, with loving than being loved, of understanding rather than being understood, of genuinely being interested in doing good without expecting any returned reward, recognition, and benefit, when people realize that complete forgiveness and selfless service are the only way—only then will everyone be really living!

Things around here are good and bad, mainly the latter. This week I had a memorial service for a young man, with under 30 days left to do here, who attended my worship services, who was kind, with a smile and made people laugh and lift them from depression, anger, and anxiety. He drowned. Another man attended one of my Sunday worship services, with his face all painted with camouflage make-up for going out on a recon. patrol. I saw him again three hours later, dead, having been shot in the head.

The men live in the most despicable of situations. They carve out holes in the hills in which to live, so that they are always damp and cold. I frankly don't know how they do it. From water shortages, they must go from 6 weeks to two months without a shower. Since they only have one set of utilities (the green uniforms we wear) they go out in patrols, get all wet from rain or river crossings, caked with mud, and must sleep in the same clothes. There are rats all over, and men are continually getting bit, and then have to get the 15 or so shots for rabbies in the stomach. There are mail delays when we don't get mail for two weeks at a time, and when it does come in, there are always many "dear Johns"—from married women! (One man came to me, almost in a state of shock. He was married 18 years, 3 children, had less than a month to do here, and no previous marriage problems, and he got a "dear John"). There is always the fear of enemy attack. There is the continual awakening at night from artillery suddenly going off at all hours of the night. There is the monotonous diet of C rations. And so on.

Yet, you would be amazed at the faith expressed here. There are evidences of genuine and deep prayer life, of reading and knowing the Bible backwards and forwards, of sacrificial concern for others. The men usually come out in large crowds for religious services. Some, of course, are merely there from fear, and their religious conviction is indeed shallow. Many have come to a religious service of worship for the first time in their lives; some have communed for the first time in two years.

I truly believe that it is when people face death, when they face the loss of all the trivia of modern day society and are face to face with the "bare essentials" of what is human, that they are the happiest, with less to gripe over and less to worry about. I think people are people only when they suffer!

Well we are fairly well blessed where we are. The monsoons that we are supposed to be suffering under haven't materialized, although we do get a week or two of solid rain now and then. The area is very beautiful—mountains, and sunsets, etc. The local tribes are hospitable and interesting. The base hasn't been attacked since 27 June. There are some local Bible translators here from Pennsylvania and I have established good relations with them, borrowing some of their Greek translation helps, so that by the time I'm finished over here I will have gone through the whole NT in Greek—I hope so, anyway.

Please write whenever you get a chance, about some of your experiences in the classroom, about your dissertation and its ideas, etc.

Faithfully yours, Ray

In a letter to his parents dated January 20, 1968, Stubbe listed a variety of minor, everyday matters with which he needed their help (making photographs out of slides he was sending home, paying his membership dues for a chaplains' association, keeping a record of the boxes he was sending home, etc.). He then remarked:

> *Last night, and at about 2 in the afternoon, just as I am writing this letter, there were B52 strikes against two suspected North Vietnamese regiments (about 3,000 or so men) to our south, about 5 miles or so. These strikes are called "arc lights" and consist of 5,000 and 10,000 pound bombs. They drop so many of them that it sounds like a real bad thunder even at this distance. So things are getting a little warmer here.*

Chaplain Stubbe, who is also featured on the cover of this book, standing in a stream off of Hill 881-South in Khe Sanh, Vietnam

His last comment could not have been more of an understatement; the next day marked the beginning of a massive siege of the Marine base at Khe Sanh by communist forces, and Stubbe and approximately 6,000 troops were pinned down for eleven weeks. On January 21, Stubbe tried to assure his parents, who he knew would have heard about the attack on the news, that he personally was fine.

Dear Folks:

First, I'm okay, not even a scratch. The casualties have been comparatively small. So don't worry.

I wrote my last entry in my log beginning Dec. 1st. Since our post office was hit this morning, I gave it to one of the pilots of one of the planes to mail via registered mail. I don't know if it will ever get home, but there's a lot in it; it's very important to me. So I hope it gets home. Please write me if it does. It's a green record book diary, covering the period 1 Dec. to today, plus a lot of personal papers.

We are, as you probably hear on the news, under attack. It's the scariest thing I've ever had to face. I awoke at 5 o'clock to the sound of incoming rockets and mortar exploding just outside my hooch! They hit our ammunition dump, and rounds of ammunition were flying all day long. Practically half the base is in ruins, but the casualties were very few because everyone got in bunkers. The only casualties were from the lines on the perimeter of the base from Hill 861. I am writing this as the sun is setting today. I don't know if you will ever receive this, but I must write it anyway.

The base is quite safe. The airstrip wasn't harmed, and planes keep coming and going. We still have our artillery for counter-mortar attacks. My hooch's well-built, sturdy. We have a lot supporting us. So don't worry.

I feel I'm needed here. I give my every waking moment for these men. They are basically good men, but not particularly religious as such, although I'm quite sure many prayed today! Yet I love them all, and give my daily life for them, and I do it not for personal satisfaction or companionship or a sense of personal accomplishment, but because I feel this is God's will.

You of course know my love for you both and grandad and all—Peg and Jeane, Jackie, Henry—everyone, but especially you and grandma. I have not always been a good son and I know I've caused you grief at times, unsureness and anxiety at other times. But I've always loved all of you very deeply.

Well, there's really not too much more to say in this situation—I've recorded all the details of everything in my log.

Love,
Ray

President Lyndon B. Johnson ordered that the base be saved at all costs, and tens of thousands of American and South Vietnamese troops were rushed to Khe Sanh. The North Vietnamese were repelled in early April, but hundreds of Americans were killed and an estimated 1,500 to 2,500 were wounded. *(Ironically, the base was closed down only months later.)* Stubbe survived the battle for Khe Sanh, and in a letter to his parents written after he was out of harm's way, he mentioned how close he had come to dying.

> So many things happened at Khe Sanh—it's good I didn't write earlier—practically anything I might write would either sicken or scare you. But that's all past now. I must say the good Lord was very merciful and gracious. I didn't even receive a cut or bruise. But there for a while I was having very close calls every day. One noon, while eating brunch in my hooch, an incoming round went into my wall—through four feet of dirt, 3 feet of sandbags, and bent my steel walls held up by u-shaped engineering stakes—it was a dud!

Stubbe returned to Wisconsin in January 1969 and stayed in the military for another sixteen years. He still preaches occasionally at his old church and ministers to the homebound and others in need.

Specialist Fourth Class Ron "Butch" Livergood Writes to His Parents About Being Overcome with Guilt After Shooting a Viet Cong Soldier

Before heading into a war zone, troops often express their desire to kill as many enemy forces as possible—and, indeed, that is what they are trained to do. But some combatants discover that taking the lives of other human beings can be an intense and even traumatic experience, especially if they came face-to-face with these individuals before killing them. Ron "Butch" Livergood, a twenty-year-old specialist fourth class serving near Ben Luc, Vietnam, sent the following letter to his parents in Garrett, Indiana, after confronting an enemy soldier. He was so torn up about the incident that he could not even write to his wife, Linda, about it.

Feb. 14, 1968

Dear Mom and Dad

Hi folks, Well I am sorry I havent wrote to you in quite a while, but if you been listen too news you could pretty well figer out. Sigon was hit heavy and we were to. So they have been keeping us busy during day and night. We were mortared last night and about 4 days ago. Two of the fellows in the Company were wounded but nothing to serious. Now don't you start worrying about me I am O.K. a little nervos but O.K.

I am not worried that much anyway I been reading the Bible off and on and it helps a lot. I think God is protecting me as much as he can. I finally got some film for my camra and I been taking pictures like mad. Mom I don't know if I should tell you this or not, but I have to tell somebody and I can't tell Linda because she would worrie to much, and I think you might be able to take it better than her. I think I might have killed a person but I am not sure, we were fired at and I seen some men running with rifles so I opened fire on them and one of them fell to the ground. I just pray to God for forgiveness.

It shook me up quite a bit but I am feeling better now, because we went out to where I seen him go down. We found blood but nobody. I am glad of that. Well I am glad I got that off my chest I feel better now. I just hope you can forgive me.

Mom I don't know if I should tell you things that happen over here or not because not to many of the guys write home about it. But the pressure builds up in me and I just have to tell somebody. If Linda if knew she might not be able to live with me knowing that her husband has killed a person. Well I change the subject. Hows all the kids back home fine I hope. Tell everyone I send my love and Ill be home in 327 days. I love you both, and I will write more later

Love
Butch
Your Son in Vietnam

P.S. Write as often as possible mail call is all I have to look forward to.

Fortunately, Livergood survived the war and returned to the States in late 1968.

After Visiting "The Wall" in Washington, D.C., John Campbell Writes a Letter to a Friend He Lost in Vietnam

For those who have never experienced combat firsthand, it can be diffi-
cult to understand the capricious brutality of warfare and the sacrifices
that military personnel are asked to make. Veterans of the war in Viet-
nam, in particular, not only had to endure some of the worst fighting
and hardships imaginable, they returned to a country that did not em-
brace them as it had troops from other conflicts. The nation's first formal
recognition of these extraordinary men and women came in 1982, when
the Vietnam Veterans Memorial—better known as "The Wall"—was
constructed in Washington, D.C. Like many veterans, John "Soup"
Campbell came to the memorial to pay tribute to the buddies he had lost
in the war, and on June 8, 1985, he wrote a letter to one of them: Eddie

Photograph by Andrew Carroll

The Vietnam War 103

Van Every Jr., who was killed at the age of twenty-two. And while Camp-
bell knew that his friend had left this world, he looked forward to seeing
him in the next one.

June 8, 1985

Dear Eddie,

Although it's been fifteen years since you've been gone, it feels like it could have been fifteen days. Many times I have regretted not getting to know you better than I did. There was a quiet, sensitive goodness about you. You were one of the guys that had been with the unit awhile and was getting "short." I knew about your girl, your Mom & Dad and that you wanted to put your time in and get home. If anyone knew you at all, they like you a lot.

I'll never forget being awakened at 3 that morning by the hysterical crying of Denny Newbill and Jerry Hall. "One of our guys is dead!" was all I could get out of Newbill. When Jerry told me it was you, I can remember demanding an answer—"Oh God, Why? Why any of us? Why Eddie?" I never did get any concrete answers. Our whole company felt a tremendous loss. When I left in August, there was still a sense of grief around. Things never did get back to "normal."

I hope you don't mind, but recently I made contact with your parents. They've moved twice and are now retired in Missouri, trusting in the Lord that you are at peace. They can't afford to travel much, so I've sent them pictures of the Memorial and your name. They're good people, too. I hope to meet them some day.

For years, I felt your life, as well as the other 58,000 lives, was wasted and anyone who wasn't there, could not or would not understand what we went through. That's changing now. People are beginning to realize that we were doing our jobs and doing them well. We had to pay the price and until recently, we were the ones tagged as losers, not our government. So if your names on this wall make it harder to send guys half way around the world to die, then maybe it wasn't a total waste.

I love you, brother. I pray some day we can welcome each other home. Peace.

John "Soup" Campbell

⇒ The Gulf War ⇒

U.S. Marine Corps Captain Steve Belgum, Serving in Operation Desert Storm, Receives a Letter from a Woman Named Lynda Severson—and Their Ensuing "Pen Pal" Exchange Leads to a Surprising Conclusion

To a soldier, Marine, airman, or sailor serving abroad, few things can boost morale like a handwritten letter. These messages of support offer a tangible connection to friends and loved ones, and even mail from a total stranger can be a lift to the spirits. Lynda Severson, a twenty-six-year-old human resources manager working in Minneapolis, did not have any family in the armed forces. But after the United States launched Operation Desert Storm to liberate Kuwait in January 1991, she sent the following letter to a Marine named Steve Belgum on January 27 to let him know that, although they had never met, she was grateful for his service to our nation.

Dear Steve—

I'm a friend of Linnea Hanson's, who is a flight attendant for Northwest and flew troops to Germany over the holidays; she asked that I write to let you know you're in our thoughts & prayers . . . Hopefully, you're not an English Major as the previous sentence was definitely a run-on.

I was given a list of twelve names to write to. I've distributed the other eleven names to my co-workers & Bible study friends. You see, your name came w/ a reference. Someone under your command said some very <u>nice</u> things about you! Isn't that great to know your peers think very highly of you!

The same two groups of people mentioned above: My coworkers @ Daytons (a leading retail firm in MPLS & the Midwest) and my Bible study friends (PCWN—Professional Christian Women's Network) sent Christmas cards, wrapped tins of Christmas cookies, books, etc. to some troops in Saudi Arabia. We are all behind you and your efforts!!

Presently, I'm on a plane en route to Minneapolis. I just spent 4 days visiting my brother, Mark, in Butte, Montana! We both love to downhill ski!! Tomorrow, it's back to work . . .

Being I've been told your age (29, right?), I'll let you know I'm 26 (27 in May). I graduated from the University of Texas at Dallas in Public and Political Communications.

If you have an opportunity to write back, I'd appreciate hearing from you . . . Again, I want to tell you how much we all appreciate what you're doing in the Persian Gulf. Hopefully, you'll all be back to America soon! May God Bless You and keep you in His care!

In Friendship, Lynda (Severson)

Belgum replied soon after he received Severson's letter.

Dear Lynda,

Hi! Happy Valentine's Day! Linnea told me you would be writing. Thank you for keeping all of us servicemen and women in your thoughts and prayers. We really appreciate the support; it does make a difference over here.

No, I am not an English major. In fact, I studied Business and minored in Entrepreneurship at Seattle Pacific University and graduated in 1983. Seattle Pacific is a small private school in Seattle, WA. Regardless of your writing, I would not criticize it because then you would tell me how sloppy my handwriting is. So, I cheated this time and used the computer. . . .

I would like to be as specific in telling you what I do but I can't talk much about it right now because the operations I am assigned to are ongoing. I am an assistant Operations Officer and work for a LtCol who is the Ops Off. Basically I help plan future operations, train Marines who work in the same section that I do, and stand watch daily . . .

Yes, you got it right. I am 29 but soon to be 30 years old (March 31). Ouch, that sounds old, doesn't it? Just kidding. I plan on being in shape to run triathlons in my 60's. Unfortunately, we have little time or facilities to stay in any decent shape . . .

Well, that's about enough rambling to bore you to death by now. If you care to write me back, I would like to hear from you. Also, I really like pictures. I'll see if I can get one to send you. Could you send me a picture? Thanks.

Take care, Steve

> *From this simple exchange, a friendship blossomed. On Belgum's birthday, Severson sent him a card with some photographs of herself. "Steve—Wherever this finds you, I hope your day is wonderful!! Happy 30th Birthday!! Happy Easter!! w/ a b-day hug, Lynda." And on the opposite side, Severson wrote: "Thanks for your nice letter! All the events in the Persian Gulf have certainly changed since you wrote! Praise the Lord!! . . . I'm curious to know where you live—CA? WA? What is your next assignment? . . . Here are a few photos to keep or throw away." Belgum replied on April 17.*

Dear Lynda:

Thanks for the birthday card and the pictures! It got turned around in the mail system and so I did not receive it until I had been back at work for a few days. I guess I should back up. On the 2nd of April we finally left Saudi Arabia. . . . My sister and mother met me at Camp Pendleton at 3:00 am when I returned. Wow, what a great homecoming! They had my apartment all decorated up and had already filled the refrigerator for me. I have been relaxing since then.

Lynda, I have to say this: you are gorgeous! I would love to meet you. Throw your pictures away—are you kidding? . . .

I live in Escondido which is in San Diego county. I drive 35 minutes to work at Camp Pendleton, the large Marine base on the coast just north of San Diego. . . . My sister and brother (both younger), and my mother all live within 2 & ½ hours drive from my place. We all had dinner my second night back. The first weekend I stayed at my sister's place and met her friends.

You are an active person. Besides work you have a second job, are involved at church and a Professional Women's club, and stay in shape. That's a lot. I am also very active. Besides work I workout daily, sometimes twice a day, stay current on the news, and continue learning a second language (Spanish). During a previous tour in South Carolina I was in the Big Brothers/Big Sisters Program. My little brother, there, is Robbie who is now 14 years old. We had a great time together every week. I miss spending time with him. . . .

Thanks again for the card. I did have a good birthday but I am now over the hill (just kidding!) . . . Please call me if you would like to.

Warmly, Steve

Severson took him up on the offer, and they began phoning each other regularly. In July 1991, Belgum went to visit Severson in Minnesota, and he wrote to her immediately after getting back to San Diego.

Dear Lynda (bucket of sunshine),

I'm missing you already! . . . I'm sorry I couldn't say goodbye to you at the gate, but I jumped on the plane with 13 minutes to spare, just barely before they seated the standby's. What a whirlwind weekend! . . . What a great way to start off our friendship! I still have a hard time believing how much we did in 3 days.

Can you believe we hit it off that well for having talked via just letters and a few phone calls? Amazing. I had such a great time with you. You are relaxed, self-confident, self-sufficient, believe in God, not to mention great looking and tons of fun to be with!!

Continuing our friendship will be frustrating. Minneapolis is so far from San Diego! 3½ hours on a plane plus a 40 minute drive to the airport. But as I said at brunch when we were at "Windows of Mpls", just take it a day at a time. Who can predict the future? No one that I know . . . So, when can you visit me in S. D.? After August 20th, but not September 20th to October 15th.

As little as I know you, I like you and want to get to know you better.

Warmly, Steve

Two months later, Severson went to San Diego, and her trip was equally as enjoyable.

Dearest Steve,

Wow! What a fabulous time in S.D.! Thanks for being such a great host! I'm very impressed w/ your home, neighbors, brother, friends (Tom & Bob), and more on the personal side—your honesty, intellect, closeness to your family, athletic abilities, interest in travel, high self esteem, great body, handsome face—I could go on and on . . . (Beautiful voice!)

As you know, I made it to the gate and on the airplane in plenty of time. I started reliving the wonderful weekend and thought about how I already missed you . . . Then, I looked out the window and noticed an "Oakley" T-Shirt. Hey! I know that guy!! How nice of you to see me off! It meant a lot. Leave it to you to surprise me once again !!! If I'm not mistaken, you were singing, right? I couldn't make out the words but I love when you sing to me!

You'll never guess who I'm sitting next to on the plane right now, a Marine! He just finished his basic training @ Campen and is flying to LaCrosse for a 10 day leave before he returns to your base. His girlfriend flew out for graduation so she's on the aisle side of him. His name is Pvt. Morgan (from WI) in case you have anything to do w/ his next phase of training. . . . His eyes lit up when I said your name Capt. Belgum. "He's a Captain?"

I know some people who use that title on all their correspondence, check info, personal things, etc. and am glad you're humble about it! "Those who think too highly of themselves shall be humbled, but those who humble themselves shall be exalted."—that's from somewhere in the Bible. And you asked about "Believe and be satisfied." I know that's not directly from the Bible; however, its base is biblical. I don't know the author. I'm glad you asked about that article.

I sometimes wonder if I make you uncomfortable w/the Bible verses and articles I send. I have no intention of pushing my beliefs on you . . . but you've been a Christian since you were nine and . . . once a Christian always a Christian . . . It's great to question beliefs and Scripture itself. It's ok to fall away from practicing any religion for a period of time but I believe a majority of those people rededicate their lives to Christ at some point again. It's easy for me to talk to you about this because the spiritual part of my life is more important to me than anything and I'm glad you recognize and respect my beliefs. (In fact, you mentioned that it's something you like most about me.)

Well, I'm back in Mpls again . . . I am truly amazed at how well we got along again—we're two for two! 2 Great wknds to 2 possible total. I know that two wknds out of my 27 years of life (and your 30) aren't a whole lot, but we do have something special! I know a good thing when I see it!

Severson knew that the relationship was getting serious, and on October 17 she wrote the following late-night letter candidly describing the internal conversation she was having with herself and expressing the emotions she was feeling.

Dearest Steve . . .

It's interesting how my mind thinks through so many options every time we're together . . . We have so much fun together . . . I'd love to spend more time w/Steve . . . distance is "safer" for our relationship—I can continue to be involved in all my activities . . ."Distance makes the heart grow fonder" . . . I'd like to move to CA between Christmas and June '92 . . .

At this stage of the game we need to say what's on our minds and in our hearts . . . It would be nice to be married—Steve says he wants to be married—he doesn't know to who—wouldn't it be nice if it was me! . . . Be realistic! You've spent very few days of your lives together (10 to be exact). How can you know at this point if you're meant to be together forever—forever is a long time . . . I won't make vows I can't keep! But in our "quality" days together we've learned how great we are for each other—people say we "click". I pray that the Lord wants us to be together . . . would enjoy a military lifestyle—It would give me the variety I've always appreciated in my life . . . we'd move, meet new friends, join new churches, get involved in USMC social activities & duties, etc . . . I will always be the eternal optimist . . . our relationship is going to work . . .

I think we think alike, right? Do any of these things cross your mind? I believe they do. I look forward to seeing you in December! In the meantime, my mind will continue to have conversations with my heart . . . Thanks for bringing so much joy into my life! (Sounds like something my mom said.) May God keep you in His special care!! I miss you!

Love and hugs, Lynda

As it turned out, Belgum was thinking many of the same thoughts.

Dear Lynda . . .

Thanks for being so honest with me.; that really means a lot to me. . . . It is your decision on whether you move here to California and when. I said before and I will say again, I want you to move here to San Diego! . . . .

Knowing each other for 5 months is not much. Selfishly, I want you to move out here sooner so I can be with you more. Obviously, that is only 5 months, and then a 7 month absence. I understand that. . . . I don't want to sound harsh but I committed myself to a minimum 12 month period of solid dating. Do you think that is unrealistic? Considering this is the precursor to choosing a lifetime partner, I don't think so.

Well, there you have it. I have laid my soul bare on some very personal issues. I would not have taken the time to answer your questions carefully if I did not care for you. I care for you very much. I can't bring myself to use the word "love", at least not yet! Although I would like to use that word. . . .

Thinking of You, Steve

On December 12, 1991, Severson wrote to Belgum that she was closer to making a decision about moving to California.

Dearest Steve—

This has certainly been a rough week . . . First of all I go into "withdrawal" from not seeing you. Second, I'm beginning to strongly consider a move to CA. There are numerous aspects that go into planning. . . . The Lord gives us choices and I pretty much decided to move to CA on my flight home from S.D. Now it's the pursuing of "this" and "that" which is difficult.

I've always asked the Lord to give me the desires of my heart—now He's blessed me w/you! I've always trusted Him enough to give all my worries and burdens over to Him. Now I struggle because my faith seems weak . . . Please pray for me and this major decision in my life! . . .

Miss you! Love you! Lynda

Severson moved to California in January, and after the two dated for another eleven months (Belgum was deployed to Okinawa, Japan, from May through November 1992), Belgum proposed on November 11—Veterans Day. They married Memorial Day weekend in May 1993 and now have two sons, Mark and Zachary. Steve remained in the Marine Corps Reserve, and on February 14, 2003, he received orders to go back on active duty. Just weeks before their ten-year anniversary and fearing that her husband would be sent to Iraq, Lynda wrote the following letter on March 3, 2003.

Dearest Steve—

I have always wondered if I'd ever be one of those military wives who'd embrace her husband and say "good-bye" as tears streamed down her face . . . while he left to serve our country.

Well, here we are, ten years into our marriage and it's time for me to send you off to a bigger cause beyond our family . . . I'm very proud of you for your twenty year dedication to the United States Marine Corps!

I realize that becoming a single mom for an uncertain amount of time is the sacrifice I'm willing to pay for gaining our American freedom back. I will pray continuously for your safety! May the Lord give you wisdom, strength and power to carry out His will.

Lynda

Ultimately, Steve did not go overseas. Instead, he served at Camp Pendleton helping young Marines with their deployments to and from Iraq.

Steve, Lynda, Zachary, and Mark Belgum. The photograph was taken just after September 11, 2001.

The War on Terrorism

**Marine Corps First Lieutenant Seth Moulton,
in a Lighthearted Letter to a Priest Back
in the States, Writes About His Favorite
Chaplain Aboard Their Ship**

*Although the subject of faith often inspires somber or pensive letters,
many troops also share humorous thoughts and experiences when they
write about God, religion, or the chaplains in their unit. While en route
to the Middle East on the USS* Belleau Wood *with the 11th Marine Expeditionary Unit, twenty-five-year-old First Lieutenant Seth Moulton
wrote to priests and chaplains who were also friends and mentors back in
Massachusetts, where he was raised. Moulton handwrote the following
letter to a priest he knew in college.*

June 25, 2004

Dear Father Bob,

I don't think I can describe the excitement that attends mail call aboard ship or in
country. It is always good to hear from you and learn of your latest work and trav-
els, but all the more so when I am away myself.

Life aboard the USS Belleau Wood en route to the Middle East has been just
fine. I really do enjoy being at sea—it must be my Marblehead upbringing, because it's not a sentiment widely shared among the Marines. To me, the tight
quarters, mediocre food, and long work days are acceptable sacrifices in the name

Father Shaughnessy and Seth Moulton in Iraq, August 2003

of an overall slower pace of life that allows for more time to read, write, and watch movies than I ever find at home. When you don't have to commute to work, run errands, do the dishes, or go out nights, there's suddenly a lot more time in every day. . . .

Church services aboard ship are quite a topic in and of themselves. The Catholic Chaplains in the Navy are far and away the best, and we have two good ones aboard the Belleau Wood. Father Shaughnessy is everybody's favorite. He's a big guy who grew up in a blue-collar family from Worcester. Every night just before taps is announced at 10 pm, they have an evening prayer over the ubiquitous announcement system. Somehow Father Shaughnessy has worked out a deal whereby he bucks what must be a regular rotation among the chaplains, because he ends every one of his prayers with, "And sportsfans, you'll be glad to know that the Red Sox won tonight." If things are going well, that's followed by "and for you New Yorkers, the Yankees lost." Unfortunately, it means that he hasn't been saying too many prayers of late! . . .

Of course, all this will be a thing of the past in a few weeks when we hit the ground in Kuwait. Then it's a couple weeks of training before we convoy north to Iraq. I can't say any more about where we're going, but it should certainly be interesting. Everybody seems anxious to get on with things.

Duty calls, as I have to work on another brief in preparation for our work in Iraq. I hope all continues well with you, and thanks again for writing.

Sincerely yours, Seth

≡⊶ **In an E-Mail to Friends and Family, Major Clint Sundt Expresses His Wonder at the History of the Land in Which He Is Serving**

"I have been in Iraq for three months now," U.S. Army Major Clint Sundt, a thirty-four-year-old National Guard infantryman, wrote in his journal while stationed in Balad in May 2004. "Because of this, I will never see my son blow seven candles on a birthday cake. I will not be with my wife on our 13th anniversary. I will not be there when my youngest son says his first full sentence, or my daughter finishes the third grade." As hard as it was to be separated from his family, Sundt was emboldened by his faith, and he concluded his journal by saying: "God has sent me here for a bigger purpose. Maybe, just maybe, my sacrifices will glorify him and make a difference for someone I never knew three months ago. I must put my faith in the hands of the Lord and be obedient to his will. It is for that obedience that I pray." Sundt's e-mails home also focused on both the challenges of being overseas and how meaningful the experience was to him. In one of his earliest messages back to his family and friends, he offered his first impressions of Iraq.

Hello all! Hope this finds you all well. I want to begin this update by saying thanks to all of you who replied to me and sent words of support. I can't tell you enough how much that lifts my spirits, and encourages me to continue to have a good attitude and approach to this mission. . . .

We have been assigned to a northern part of Iraq. I was selected to travel to our destination as part of a small advanced party detachment. There were only three of us selected to do this. Our job was to get to our destination and start making coordination and liaisons with the units already on the ground. To do this, we flew.

We flew on a Chirpa-23. This is a small, 8 passenger prop Army airplane. This flight was one of the coolest flights I have ever taken . . . I couldn't help but think about all the history that was below me. Iraq is the place where the world began. The Tigris and Euphrates Rivers meet at the place known as the birthplace of civilization. This region is also the place where Abraham migrated from (Abraham is claimed to be the father of the Hebrew / Jewish Nation (Isaac) as well as the Muslim/Islam nation—(Ishmael)). One of my goals this year while in Iraq is to read the entire Bible (chronological order, NIV). Well, I just happen to be reading the book of Genesis right now!! Genesis is all about this time era, and its major events. So to actually see this land, and read about its history is absolutely fascinating! The other thing I couldn't help but think about was the history of the war. I could see tracks in the sand, dug out tank fighting positions, and the axis of advance where our brave armed forces had gone before us to liberate this country. It was an amazing sight. . . .

The tent we were assigned was not much to write home about. It was a tiny tent with six bunk beds in it (to sleep 12 total people). . . . The tent was just like the one Hawkeye, BJ and Charles from MASH lived in, except smaller! Well, we knew we couldn't change things for the night, so we bedded down at about 2200 (10:00 pm). At 0014 I awoke to the most terrifying moment of my life. I could hear a thunderous, loud sound of the rockets and artillery impacting outside. The percussion from the rounds detonating was so close, you could feel it in your stomach. I jumped/ fell from my bed (in a dazed state), and began fumbling around in the dark trying to find my clothes, shoes, Kevlar, weapons and body armor. Finally, after what seemed to be an eternity, I found my gear and exited the tent. Unknown to us until that very moment, there were no bunkers near our tent. We were forced to huddle next to some concrete barrier walls, and hope that a round would not impact in our direct vicinity. As we crouched behind the barrier in the pitch dark night, we began to hear small arms machine gun fire. This was very confusing. We had no idea where the shooting was coming from, who was shooting at whom, or if they were headed our way. All we could do was increase our sense of awareness, lock and load our weapons, and keep our heads down.

The mortar and artillery fire lasted for about thirty minutes. It was undoubtedly the longest thirty minutes of my life. Once the all clear signal was given, we went back to our tent, and tried to sleep the rest of the night. As I lay there after the attack, I couldn't help but think about how grateful I was to the Lord for protecting me, and allowing me to survive everyday that I had so far. I never realized how good life is. I guess it takes a life changing experience to jar your thoughts and thankfulness. I am grateful. I thank the Lord everyday for allowing me to live. . . . it truly is a blessing.

I also could not help but think about the experiences and risks the soldiers before us endured. My experiences to date are nothing compared to the ones who have gone before me. Not just here in Iraq, but in all the wars before this one as well. I'm also thankful to those Veterans for what they did for our Country. I look forward to thanking the ones I know in person. . . .

God Bless, Clint

Sundt served for eleven months and returned to his family in Arizona in May 2005.

⟜⟝ The Day Before He Died, Journalist David Bloom E-mails His Wife and Daughters to Say That, No Matter What Happens, "I am at Peace"

In an unprecedented effort to show Americans firsthand the courage and bravery of our nation's fighting forces, the Pentagon allowed hundreds of journalists to be "embedded" within individual military units serving in Operation Iraqi Freedom. These reporters encountered many of the same hardships and risks that U.S. troops did, as they all rushed—without sleep and under enemy fire—at breakneck speed toward Baghdad. And the terrible reality of these risks became evident in the early weeks of the invasion when two reporters died covering the war. The first was Michael Kelly, who was killed when the Humvee he was riding in crashed on April 3, 2003. Just three days later, the distinguished NBC News correspondent David Bloom died of a blot clot (also known as a pulmonary embolism), which was caused by the long hours he spent crammed inside a tank recovery vehicle, often with his knees pressed up against his chest.

In an e-mail home written only the day before he died, the thirty-nine-year-old Bloom expressed to his wife, Melanie, how much he loved her and their three young daughters. And, especially in the context of all that he was witnessing in a war zone, he emphasized his devotion to God and the things that matter most in life.

It's 10 a.m. here Saturday morning, and I've just been talking to my soundman Bob Lapp about his older brother, whom he obviously loves and admires very much, who's undergoing chemotherapy treatment for Leukemia. Here Bob is—out in the middle of the desert—and the brother he cares the world for—who had been the picture of health, devoted to his wife and kids, is dying.

Bob can't wait to be home to be with him, and I can't wait to be home to be with all of you. You can't begin to fathom—cannot begin to even glimpse the enormity—of the changes I have and am continuing to undergo. God takes you to the depths of your being—until you are at rock bottom—and then, if you turn to him with utter and blind faith, and resolve in your heart and mind to walk only with him and toward him, picks you up by your bootstraps and leads you home.

I hope and pray that all my guys get out of this in one piece. But I tell you, Mel, I am at peace. Deeply saddened by the glimpses of death and destruction I have seen, but at peace with my God, and with you. I know only that my whole way of looking at life has turned upside down—here I am, supposedly at the peak of professional success, and I could frankly care less. Yes, I'm proud of the good job we've all been doing, but—in the scheme of things—it matters little compared to my relationship with you, and the girls, and Jesus. There is something far beyond my level of human understanding or comprehension going on here, some forging of metal through fire.

I shifted my book of daily devotions and prayers to the inside of my flak jacket, so that it would be close to my heart, protecting me in a way, and foremost in my thoughts. When the moment comes when Jim or John—or Christine or Nicole or Ava or you—are talking about my last days, I am determined that they will say 'he was devoted to his wife and children and he gave every ounce of his being not for himself, but for those whom he cared about most—God and his family.' Save this note. Look at it a month from now, a year from now, 10 years from now, 20 years from now. You cannot know now—nor do I—whether you will look at it with tears, heartbreak and a sense of anguish and regret over what might have been, or whether you will say—he was and is a changed man, God did work a miracle in our lives.

But I swear to you on everything that I hold dear—I am speaking the truth to you. And I will continue to speak the truth to you. And, not to be trite, but that will set me free. God bless you, Melanie. I love you and I know that you love me. Please give the girls a big hug—squeeze 'em tight—and let them know just how much their daddy loves and cares for them. With love and devotion, Dave.

After Being Asked by His Father if He Believes in God, Staff Sergeant Brian T. Craig Writes Home from Afghanistan with a Heartfelt Answer
&
A Wounded and Grieving Staff Sergeant, Jeff Pugmire, also Serving in Afghanistan, Vents to His Wife About the Loss of Several of His Closest Friends

U.S. troops serving today have more ways of communicating with the home front than any other generation of military personnel. Satellite phones, e-mail, and other high-speed forms of communication make it possible for servicemen and women in even the remotest parts of the world to talk or correspond instantaneously with their loved ones back in the States. But when they have something important to say, they often still put pen to paper and write a letter home. In early April 2002, twenty-seven-year-old Brian T. Craig, a staff sergeant in the Army's 710th Explosives Ordnance Disposal (EOD) unit, phoned his dad in Houston, Texas, from Afghanistan to tell him that he was doing well. Craig's father, Arthur, was a pastor, and he knew that his son's faith in God and Jesus Christ had waned at times. During their conversation,

Pastor Craig asked his son, "Brian, how is your walk with the Lord?"
Right at that moment there was interference and the line went dead. The
answer to his father's question was so important to Brian that he decided
to respond to his father with an actual handwritten letter.

08 Apr 02

Dear Dad,

You have asked about my walk with Christ on the phone. I just wanted to write and
let you know how things are going. I just started the book you sent "The Four Pil-
lars of Man's Heart". It seems as though every book that you send is an answer to
my prayers. God has really blessed me with both a great father and mother. I am
so fortunate to have two people that I can always come to for advice. Thank you.

It is strange that of all my experiences in life, that here in Afghanistan I have
really started to grow spiritually. The bible study that I was having with the group
of guys before was an answered prayer. When I come home I will start to look for

Brian Craig in Houston, Texas, holding his nephew
Samuel before Craig embarked for Afghanistan

a weekly bible study. I realize how important it is. I also realize how important prayer is. The book "Fresh wind, Fresh Fire" was great.

I have my good days and my bad days. I guess that is to be expected. I will do so good for a couple of days and then falter. I know as I continue to grow in the Lord, that my good days will outnumber my bad. I know that you pray for me and I thank you. Just know that God is answering your prayers concerning me.

I never thought that I could grow in my relationship with God around the people that I work with. I read in one of the books as Christians we know there is a hole we just don't know how deep it goes. I want to know how deep it goes. I don't know if I said that right, but you know what I mean. My life is changing and I like it. I think that the guys I work with know that I am different. I just pray that I make a difference in their lives. I pray that I am a good example. Pray for me that I may be a good example of a man of Christ. Pray that I make the right decisions, say the right things, act the way that I should as a Christian.

Thank you for your wisdom. Thank you for being the great parents that you are. Thank you for all that you do for me. Thank you for being a role model. Thank you for being not only parents but great friends. I love you and Mom so much.

Love,
Brian

Tragically, this was the last letter that Brian ever wrote to his father. Exactly one week later, Craig and four other soldiers were in the process of destroying a cache of rockets just outside of Kandahar, Afghanistan, when a terrorist detonated a hidden bomb near where they were standing. Only one of the soldiers, Staff Sergeant Jeff Pugmire, survived. "I really don't know what to say right now," Pugmire e-mailed his wife, Jennie, back in California on April 20 from a hospital in Germany. "Three of my very dear friends paid the ultimate price for our freedom," he continued.

They laid down their lives on the alter of freedom and I should have been with them. I don't know why God has called them home and not me. And I feel so very guilty for that. Why is my life worth anymore than theirs?? Why did they die and I live?

The next day Pugmire wrote a longer e-mail articulating the many thoughts that were going through his head about the deaths of Brian Craig, Justin Galewski, Jamie Maugans, and Aaron Daniel Romero.

Sun, 21 Apr 2002

Hello my lover,

I guess that I don't really need to talk to you about the explosion as I have already talked to you and you should have gotten an email from me already. In my previous email I talked a little about my feeling about what has happened and I just need to get it out. I didn't want to do it on the phone, so as to keep you in good spirits, but I just can't quit thinking about Justin, Brian, Jamie and Aaron. I think about their families and how incredibly hard this will be for them. Hopefully they have some belief in God or basis in the gospel, as that I believe is the only way they will make sense of this terrible and horrendous incident. I pray for them honey, I really do. I pray for Justin's little children, they will never have a chance to know him. How hard will that be, how terribly hard.

I have so many feelings welled up inside of me right now. Feelings of anger, hate, sorrow, elation and I don't know how to explain it . . . I am so very angry that they are gone. If I swore honey, I would say nasty and mean things. I am angry at the Afghan people. We didn't ask to come here, we didn't ask to die here, but our Commander in Chief asked us to because we love our freedom and our country—we gladly put our lives on the line, every single day. We don't complain or grumble, we just do what was asked of us by our President and you know what Jennie, most of the people in America don't understand it. They really don't understand why we are here. We have the best country in the world, and because they called us we are here. We're here to make sure no one else will fly planes into buildings and kill innocent people. I think after that happened, we now begin to realize what some people face every day. Look at what happens in Israel. We know how they feel, they know how we feel. I can tell you though, that we don't do it for money or for fame or fortune . . . (heaven knows I will never be rich), we do it for one another. For the men and women that are next to us. For our President, for our families, but most of all Jennie, I do it for you and our beautiful little girls. I do it so they can be safe and not have to worry about the evilness in the world. I am here because I believe in Democracy and that our freedom is worth the lives of my fallen brothers. I would gladly give mine in its defense.

All that aside, honey, I'm still angry and frustrated. I am so happy to be alive, I don't know how to tell you what I am feeling right now. I don't know how to express it to you, I only hope that deep inside you can connect with me and understand. Pray for their families Jennie, pray for them. I hope that I can meet with them and tell them that they didn't die in vain. I was going to get into the details, but I just don't have it in me yet. Maybe tomorrow. I cannot wait until we can be together. Give the girls my love. I will try and call tonight.

I love you,
Jeff

Terry A. Ward, the Mother of a Fallen Hero in Afghanistan, Asks Another Mother, Gloria Caldas, to Help Her Through Her Anguish
&
Caldas Replies

On September 20, 2004, Terry Ward had just returned home after doing errands when a family friend rushed over to the house and told her to go inside and wait by the telephone for an urgent message. When the phone finally rang, it was Ward's daughter-in-law, Tammy, calling to tell her the awful news that Staff Sergeant Tony B. Olaes—Ward's thirty-year-old son and Tammy's husband—had been killed in Afghanistan. Olaes was a Green Beret combat medic, and he and another soldier, Robert S. Goodwin, were shot during an ambush in Shkin, Afghanistan. A memorial page for Olaes appeared on the Internet, and while reading through the comments Ward came across a tribute posted by a total stranger that moved her deeply.

To Tony's Family and Friends: On behalf of the Blanco-Caldas family, we send our sincerest condolences. We share the same loss . . . the same pain. Our prayers are with you in this most difficult time and we thank you for your soldier's bravery and sacrifice. Sincerely, The Family of Capt. Ernesto M. Blanco-Caldas, 82nd Airborne KIA Iraq 12/28/2003.

Gloria Caldas (The Big Ern's Mom) of San Antonio, TX

Ward felt an immediate connection to Caldas, and she sent her the following e-mail:

DEAR GLORIA,

THANK YOU SO MUCH FOR THE CONDOLENCES ON THE FALLEN HEROES SITE FOR MY SON. MAY I ALSO EXPRESS MY CONDOLENCES ON THE LOSS OF YOUR OWN SON. I AM SO DEVASTATED AND I CANNOT FIGURE OUT HOW TO GO ON. HOW DO YOU MANAGE EVERY DAY?

MY SON HAD 3 YOUNG SONS, 11, 10 AND 7. HOW DO I HELP THEM? AND HIS WIFE, WHO LOVED HIM SO MUCH. I KNOW I NEED TO BE STRONG FOR THEM ALSO, BUT I AM SO SAD MYSELF.

SO SORRY TO ASK YOU THESE QUESTIONS, BUT YOU HAVE BEEN THERE ALSO, SO I KNOW YOU UNDERSTAND.

PLEASE FORGIVE THE CAPITALS, BUT I AM LEGALLY BLIND AND HAVE A HARD TIME ON THE COMPUTER, IF THE LETTERS ARE NOT BIG.

I HOPE YOU DON'T MIND ME WRITING YOU, BUT I FIGURED THAT IS WHY YOU GAVE YOUR EMAIL ADDRESS. HOPE I AM NOT RAMBLING.

I LOOK FORWARD TO HEAR-
ING FROM YOU, AND HOPE
MAYBE YOU CAN GIVE ME
SOME INSIGHT.

YOURS TRULY,
TERRY A. WARD
MOTHER OF SSG. TONY
BRUCE OLAES KIA
SEPTEMBER 20, 2004

Caldas responded right away.

Oh Terry! I know so well the pain you
are going through. I wish no one else
would have to go through what our families have experienced. During the first
several weeks after Ernie's "Homego-
ing," I fell into a black hole.

Tony B. Olaes

I guess this was the Lord's way of protecting me from the horror of the un-
thinkable. Losing a child is a bad thing. In my anger, the Lord and I had quite a
few very lively discussions! But little by little, I began to climb out of the despair
with the loving support of family, friends and my faith. Ernie was not married yet,
but he did leave a grieving fiancee who has not yet recovered. They were sched-
uled to marry on June 12th. It's now been 9 months since he was killed, I am finally able to provide support and comfort to those around me . . . his sister,
grandparents, aunts, uncles, cousins and all those who have also been deeply affected by his loss.

Normal will never be what it was before . . . we've all had to redefine "nor-
mal." Nothing will ever be the same, but you learn to just take one day at a time.
Sometimes there are bad days, sometimes worse days. But I know that as long as
I have a breath in my body, my son will live in my heart. I'm sure you feel the

same. My faith sustains me and I know that I will be reunited with him when I too go Home. I know I'm rambling, Terry.

My heart aches for you. Please get back to me. Tell me more about Tony. I'm sure your extremely proud of him, as I am of Ernie.

By His Grace, Gloria

Gloria Caldas and Terry Ward continued to send one another words of support and encouragement after their initial exchange. "JUST WANTED TO LET YOU KNOW THAT I AM THINKING OF YOU AT THIS DIFFICULT TIME," Ward wrote to Caldas after Christmas 2004. "I AM ALSO KEEPING YOU IN MY THOUGHTS AND PRAYERS AS THE ANNIVERSARY DATE OF ERNIE'S DEATH APPROACHES. JUST KNOW THAT YOU ARE NOT ALONE."

Gloria Caldas and her son, Ernie, on the balcony of his apartment near Fort Bragg, NC, the day before he embarked for Iraq. Gloria never saw her son again.

In an E-mail to Loved Ones, Lieutenant Colonel Scott Barnes Tries to Answer the Question "Where Is God?" in a Place as Violent as Iraq

Every generation of troops serving in a war zone struggles with the question, Where is God amidst such tragedy? And the military personnel deployed to Afghanistan and Iraq are no different. Frontline medics and doctors, in particular, have to face tremendous suffering on a constant basis, but many, like Lieutenant Colonel Scott Barnes, discover that their faith is nevertheless unwavering. Barnes left Fort Bragg, North Carolina, in August 2005 for Baghdad with the 86th Combat Support Hospital, and the forty-three-year-old doctor went on to treat hundreds of wounded and dying patients. On October 27, 2005, he sent the following e-mail to family and friends back in the States to describe the care they were providing not only for injured Americans, but Iraqis as well. (The ellipses within the paragraph are in the original.)

To All,

First I must apologize for the dismal communication. Most of you knew that I had deployed to Iraq in mid AUG but most of you haven't heard from me since then. I have no excuses other than being quite busy and trying to maintain communication with my wife and children when I get some free time. . . .

The work is great and terrible at the same time. The level of injuries is nothing that I have seen in this concentrated amount. I will have seen more here in a few months than I probably will see in the rest of my ophthalmology career as far as trauma goes. The Lord has been gracious and I have had some down times and been able to catch my breath . . . but for the most part my days start at 630 AM and end around 1030 PM or later. That is if I am not up through the night with a surgical case and that happens about 1–3 times a week. . . .

But I have no doubt that this is exactly where the Lord wants me to be. I am convinced that I am here for a reason. And I can see it on the faces of some of the soldiers and the Iraqi civilians on whom I operate. . . . When I tell them that I volunteered to come over here because I want to be the guy standing in the door to meet them when they get broken . . . I wanted to be a part of the greatest altruistic humanitarian effort that I believe any warfare has ever seen. We have medics that ignore bullets flying overhead just to get to a casualty; we have medevac pilots that will rush into a hot zone and won't leave "until [they] have your wounded;" we have corpsmen and orderlies that run out to the bird and transport the patients into the bays of the emergency room where medics and ER docs work tirelessly to diagnose and stablize the patient; and then the OR techs, nurses, and surgeons who work all hours to mend the broken parts; followed by the awesome nurses who continue that healing and work to mend the broken hearts of young guys whose lives have changed in an instant. I have never been involved with anything in medicine as incredible as this operation. The cause is noble and the people are the greatest team of which I have ever been a part. . . .

We also provide state of the art medical/surgical care for enemy combatants . . . even have an entire combat support hospital set up just for detainees. Can you imagine that?! One minute they are shooting at us, trying to kill us . . . and we capture them and immediately begin to minister to their injuries and illnesses. Evil Americans that we are and all! We are making a difference in the lives over here. The media has no idea what is going on or at least they chose to ignore the truth on the ground . . . there is only a small percentage of people that do not want us here . . . and just about everybody that comes in contact with the real heart of America over here, sees the incredible value. None of us want to remain here in the long run, but so many are very, very supportive of having us here in the present. Just don't believe most of what you hear on the news channels and in the papers . . . this is a very just cause, and the good is overcoming forces of evil for Iraq.

But standing in the door to work on the heroes comes at a price. It is difficult to see all the pain and suffering. The loss of limbs, eyes, and life can be overwhelming at times. But it continues and we have saves in the midst of the losses and we continue to pour our hearts into every patient because we don't know who will make it and who will not. . . . I can't go into all of them because I said I would try to keep this short.

Some of my colleagues have wondered out loud how there can be a God with all of this suffering. I just remind them that He might just be right in some of our hands and working right beside us in the ER and OR . . . how else do you explain one young sergeant with a devastating injury where nearly his whole pelvis was shot away . . . he should have died even before reaching us, but he didn't. He had such massive blood loss that he should have died before getting to the OR. But he kept living as we kept working on him and we were running out of blood to transfuse into him . . . but his heart kept going. We found guys outside and told them we needed blood and fast. Guys started lining up to donate blood in our back parking lot. Sergeants started going up to guys that weren't even in this guys unit telling them that a young sergeant was fighting for his life and needed their blood.

They started calling their buddies located at bases close to the hospital and told them to get their backsides (translation from what most sergeants really said) over here ASAP because a fellow soldier (who most of them had never even met) was going to die without their blood. Soldiers started pouring in, asking no questions except where do they go to give blood . . . they don't even know this guy, they just knew that another brother was in trouble and needed their help. They lined up in the parking lot and when their turn came, they had buddies watch their gear and weapons while they went in to donate. No questions . . . just soldiers doing what they think is just part of their job. I think about 60–70 guys ended up donating. In the US, when a patient requires 6–12 units of blood that is considered a massive transfusion and associated with a very high rate of death. This young hero required 207 units of blood (yes you read that correctly!) . . . and he lived. He was flown back to the states and back at Walter Reed Army Medical Center is still alive and off the ventilator.

Where is God . . . He is in the OR guiding the hands of the surgeons, He is in the will of the sergeants helping organize a blood drive as only they can, He is in the hearts of the soldiers who immediately rolled up their sleeves to give what they had to save a dying brother whom they don't even know. I still cannot write about this without getting choked up . . . to see the sacrifice of the soldiers, the surgeons, the field medics who initially treated this young guy. This story alone should help make it clear why I consider serving over here this to be the greatest honor of my professional career. I get to see the real heart of the American soldier and the American military medical team . . . and they are as gold. . . .

I'll write more later . . . the pictures are of the soldiers waiting to donate blood in the above story. . . .

May God Bless you as He does for me everyday, Scott

U.S. Air Force Major Sandi Douglass and His Beloved, Air Force Captain Donna Kohout, Exchange a Series of E-mails Emphasizing Their Love for One Another Despite the Hardships They Know They Will Encounter

Having one spouse in the armed forces can be difficult for any couple, but having two can make a relationship all the more challenging. Approximately one out of every six U.S. troops is female, and a significant number of them are married to fellow service members. Like their husbands, these women are courageously defending the United States in the deserts of Iraq, the mountains of Afghanistan, and at other posts throughout the world. As hard as it can be for military couples to be separated, many find that their faith helps them endure their time apart. "Sweetheart, we need to believe the truth that it is God's will that we are together," Air Force Major Sandi Douglass wrote in October 2005 to his intended, Donna Kohout, who was a captain in the Air Force. Kohout, thirty-four, had served in Iraq and was back home in New Mexico, and Douglass was deployed to Korea. He went on to write in his e-mail, which was written only days before he returned to Korea:

I think we will continue to figure out how to integrate our lives better and better as we spend more time together here in the states . . . I don't foresee a problem . . . but I don't know how you feel about this. I haven't seen any show stoppers on my side of us. Just things to adjust here and there.

What is important is that the foundational things are solid . . . we both love God and want Him to lead us thru life . . . we both want to work in the Kingdom and spend our lives in service to Him . . . we both want a spouse who loves us unconditionally the way He intends. All the rest is detail. I don't really care how you want the laundry folded or washed . . . just let me know and it will be as you wish . . . I am not going to let details get in the way of me loving you.

I love you and I love the way you love me. I think you are simply terrific and I think you are the most beautiful creature He has ever made. . . .

ILY

> "As I was driving away from the airport this morning, I realized how much I hate saying goodbye to you," Kohout e-mailed Douglass. "But until you're here again, or I'm there, you're in His care. . . . He has a lot for you to do there, and I feel selfish wanting you to myself. I'm always impressed by your ability to give unreservedly." Douglass's virtues were even more impressive to Kohout in light of all that he had suffered as a child; Sandi Douglass was actually born Richard John Sanders in a poor neighborhood in Los Angeles to a single mom who died when he was only fourteen. He was adopted by Brenda and Clem Douglass and took on their last name. At the age of twenty-one he joined the Air Force, and eighteen years later he met Kohout. They dated for more than five months before he proposed. On October 11, and after receiving an e-mail from Douglass about the imperfections of this world (especially in comparison to the majesty of the Heavenly Kingdom), Kohout sent Douglass a profound, almost poetic e-mail about the mystery of God's plans and the importance of placing their trust in His hands.

I'm beginning to realize another piece of where you get your big heart from. God's done a lot of healing, but you also had a great example in your parents. I couldn't agree more that God doesn't work in tidy, perfect little flower gardens as dramatically as He works in the vast mountain ranges of Colorado or Alaska. They're not necessarily neat and orderly—they're wild and wonderful, but beautiful just the same. There're more colors in the weaving than we can begin to

Sandi and Donna Douglass, on their honeymoon in Korea, at the Yeouido (also spelled Yoido) Full Gospel Church. With 800,000 members, it is considered one of the largest churches in the world.

imagine . . . and I think God likes to make up new colors when He runs out of ones that exist already. I think I've told you the Weaver poem, eh?

My life is but a weaving, between the Lord and me.
I cannot choose the colors; He worketh steadily.

Oft times He weaveth sorrow, and I in foolish pride
Forget He sees the upper, and I the under side.

The dark threads are as needful in the Weaver's skillful hand
As thread of gold and silver, 'neath the pattern He has planned.

Not 'til the loom is silent and the shuttles cease to fly
Will God unveil the canvas and explain the reason why.

—Author unknown

I think it's kinda neat that one of us is always awake. I was thinking about that as I did some errands earlier. There's always one of us awake to pray. Would be neater to have you here, of course, but that'll happen in time.

ILYVM.
me

On April 1, 2006, Donna Kohout and Sandi Douglass were married. Douglass had to return to Korea two days later, although he was allowed another week off before returning to work. Despite all the heartache and uncertainties of being apart, he—like his new wife—recognized how fortunate they were to have each other. Douglass wrote the following on April 26.

Dearest Sweetheart—

Ugghh!! Rough day for both of us and the beginning of our longest separation yet. But I refuse to let my joy be stolen. He has a purpose behind this and I see my role in it a little. You are right Sweetheart, I am needed here. He has a use for me still and something I need to learn. I am so sorry you have to bear the burden of this.

Remember His blessings, His wall-writing, His abundance, His protection, and our beautiful wedding and great honeymoon. They all hold the promise of a wonderful life we will and do have together.

He is using you in this too. I could not do this without you and He needs you to reach our friends there and bring them light—let them see your joy, my love—don't let the enemy steal our joy. We are married and learning together what that means and I love every moment we have—even if I can only talk to you on the phone right now.

I love you and I miss you and I want you in my life. You are and will always be my beautiful bride. I love thee.

Me

Sixty-Five Years After They First Met, Dell Myrick Writes a Poignant Love Letter to the Man She Was Fated to Marry

Since the time of the Revolution more than two centuries ago, Americans have penned war-related letters that express every conceivable human emotion, sentiment, and experience. And the motivations behind writing this correspondence are as diverse as the letter-writers themselves. Many simply want to convey their sense of love and affection for the recipient. Others want to tell an extraordinary story that might otherwise be lost or forgotten. And some hope to impart words of advice from which younger family members and generations can learn. It is rare, however, for a single missive to do all of these things at once in a truly memorable way. The following letter was written by eighty-year-old Dell Myrick on October 5, 2006, to her husband on their wedding anniversary. Her words are a powerful reminder of the importance of faith, hope, and love—particularly during those times when all three are tested.

My Dear Herman,

As our eleventh anniversary approaches I realize how blessed we have been all these years to be together. And I also realize how much we have missed all those years before.

I remember when I was just 15 years old and approaching my 16th birthday, I was standing in the hallway of our school when I heard someone say, "I wonder who the new boy is?" And I looked up to see you there on the stairway—a brown-haired, trim, blue-eyed, jean-clad boy. Then the strangest thing happened. It was almost as if something went "zing" and an electrical shock had hit me.

To cover up my feelings I replied, "I don't know but he certainly needs a hair-cut." That was not true, for your hair was not really that long. But a sense of won-derment had come over me, and I did not understand it. I know now that God was trying to tell me something, but I didn't know what.

As it turned out, you were in my brother's class and your sister Sue was in mine. So it was inevitable that we should meet. You became my brother's friend, and your sister, Susie, became one of mine. So I found out that you and your fam-ily had just moved to Alabama from Los Angeles. Since we were in the middle of the Great Depression, things were so uncertain in those days. Money was practi-cally nonexistent and only those who lived on farms, as you and I did, could be sure of plenty to eat. So you and your family were living on your grandfather's farm and you worked on it, as well as going to school, even though you were only 17 years old the following spring.

I remember an old wooden box telephone hanging on our wall, but it was not usable because the telephone company had gone bankrupt. Dad said people in the area had cut parts of the line to use for clothesline. And since we had no car there was little communication with the outside world, except for a battery radio, which we used sparingly to make the battery last longer.

Then came December 7, 1941, when we listened in shock on this same radio that the Japanese had attacked Pearl Harbor. The next day, our teacher herded us all into the auditorium where we heard that the United States had declared war on Japan. I remember thinking that you, and my brothers, would have to go to war and might be killed.

Up until this time I had been so happy on school days and on week-ends when you would walk the 6 or 7 miles to my home to see me. Although you had a Model A Ford, you seldom used it. The 10 cent a gallon gasoline was too much to spend. Anyway, we were all used to walking the dusty country roads wherever we went. My heart always leapt with joy when I would see you. Most of our dates were at home. Sometimes we would meet at church revivals or church singings, but we never discussed marriage. Times were too uncertain after the war began to plan ahead. But it seemed that there was never any doubt in our minds and hearts that we belonged together.

Boys became a scarce commodity in high school because they went off to war as soon as they graduated. I remember that day in 1943 when two cousins of mine came to visit us and persuaded me to ride back on the bus to Birmingham to visit them for a week. This was an unusual chance for me, so I went. When I came home, I learned that you had already gone into the Navy. You had come to see me but I was not there. Since we had no telephone, there was no way to call me, and I had thought you were not leaving until the next week.

I remember how I walked out of the house, ran to the end of our garden, and collapsed in tears. I sobbed so loudly that I was afraid our neighbors on the connecting farm would hear me. But I didn't care! You had left and there was no way I could make connection with you. All my crying couldn't bring you back long enough for me to say goodbye.

Then the waiting began. I prayed for a letter from you each day. The year after you graduated I was still in high school and another classmate, Al, began coming around to see me. Once he asked me to go out with his family in a boat that he and his brothers had built, then for a picnic on the lake. So I went, for life was so dull and empty at that stage. I was greatly surprised when, athough I had only been seeing him for a month, he asked me to marry him. I remember laughing and telling him that I wasn't fool enough to believe he meant it after only a month. But he kept coming around. Then he asked me if I'd just wear his class ring. So I wrote to you and asked you if you minded if I wore Al's class ring.

How could I have known that your Chief Petty Officer was telling the men that some of you would get a "Dear John" letter, and that you might as well expect it, for it was going to happen. And just at the time that I was stupid enough to ask you the question about the class ring of Al's! He had been deferred for farming at his parent's request. But one day he volunteered for the Navy and left also.

I never got the letter you wrote in reply to my letter. There was just silence!! Day after day I heard nothing. Weeks came and went and still nothing. It wasn't until I spoke with a neighbor friend that I learned, at last, why I had not heard from you for so long: One of my sisters had gotten my letter, read it, then destroyed it, and never told me!

Sue was away in college, so I wrote her and asked for your new address. This time I was watching when her reply came. I saw my sister go to the mail box and hide the letter under her arm. I grabbed it from her and demanded to know why she was taking my mail and why she had destroyed my letter from you.

She replied that she had not gotten to marry the man she loved and did not think that the rest of the children should either. Dad had told her firmly that she would be sorry if she married the guy she was dating, that he drank and that he didn't think he was suitable for her. So in her bitterness, she decided that none of the rest of us should be happy!

Now I had your address, and I could write to you. But it had been so long since I had heard from you that I decided you must not care about me anymore.

Fifty years went by, and I was living by myself in Alabama when, miraculously, I heard that you had moved to a nearby community. I couldn't believe it!

I joined a senior exercise class where you were also going. I'll admit that I had heard that you were also there. So one day I quietly entered the class and saw a slim, trim, older version of my high school sweetheart. Your hair was no longer brown, but white. In fact, there was little left of it. There were lines in your face, as there were in mine. But the same happy twinkle was in your blue eyes when you looked at me. Although we had changed in looks, the same feelings were reflected in our faces.

We began going for a cup of coffee together, then to lunch. Then to a movie. Then just to sit and talk and become reacquainted. I explained to you what had happened to your letter, and you told me about your Chief Petty Officer preparing all of you for a "Dear John" letter. And when my letter came, you thought that was your "Dear John" letter!

After we spent a year dating, we were married. I had wanted our wedding there with my Sunday School class present, and with other members of our church, family, and friends all gathered together, we said our wedding vows fifty three years after we first met!! At that moment, I knew for certain that this was what God had intended for us.

These past eleven years have been the happiest years of my life. Although I look back with regret on all the time we could have been together, I realize that God's timing is not our timing. Maybe He was saving the best for last, and if we had gone through the struggle of raising a family and the stresses of life during a period of hard times, it might have put too great a strain on our marriage.

As it is, we have been able to be together, just the two of us, and to enjoy that time alone. We have traveled to many places; Australia, New Zealand, Israel, Europe, Alaska, the Caribbean Islands, across the United States, and many other

Herman and Dell Myrick

places. We can realize now, as we have so often said, that God had wonderful plans for us all along and guided our every step back to each other. Isn't God wonderful?

Most of all, these years together have given us an appreciation of each other, and what love is all about. It is about caring for each other, greeting each day with joy because we have each other, thanking God that we have another day together, and knowing that God planned it this way.

I have just had my 80th birthday but I still feel as if I am "sweet sixteen", and all because you love and treasure me.

I love you.

Your loving wife,
Dell

Acknowledgments and Permissions

The experience of writing this book has been a blessing in itself. From the very beginning of this process, the most compassionate and amazing people have reached out to help in some essential way, and I cannot thank them enough.

First and foremost, I am indebted to my own angel, Meredith Henne, who not only helped me read through piles of mail, type in many of the letters featured in this book, and edit the manuscript, but was a constant source of moral and spiritual strength. Her love and support were invaluable, and I am very lucky to have her in my life. I also owe an enormous debt of gratitude to Meredith's friend Skyla Freeman, who told me the story about her grandmother, Dell Myrick. I don't think I could have found a more poignant or profound ending to *Grace Under Fire* than Dell's letter, and I owe it all to Skyla.

I also want to thank my mom, who was extremely encouraging about this book idea when I first proposed it and offered very helpful feedback after reading through the first draft.

My editors at Doubleday Religion, Bill Barry and Andrew Corbin, as well as Steve Cobb at WaterBrook Press, have all been a joy to work with, and they understood the spirit of this book from the very start. It is always a pleasure to work on a project with people of enormous talent and integrity, and they are truly the best. I also want to thank Darya Porat at Doubleday for all of her assistance. We could not have done all of this without her.

I am also grateful to my agent, Miriam Altshuler, for helping me find such great editors. Miriam is more than an agent, she is a dear friend whose wisdom and kind heart I cherish, and I look forward to working with Miriam on many more projects down the road.

I am eternally indebted to Father James Hamel, who also read through an early copy of the manuscript and offered great suggestions. He is a true hero (he left for

Iraq soon after I completed the final draft), and our military—and nation—are lucky to have him serving his country and the Lord.

Megan Smolenyak Smolenyak, author of an incredible book titled *Honoring Our Ancestors,* is a brilliant genealogist (and close friend) who very generously helped me track down several veterans with whom I had lost contact over the years, and I cannot thank her enough.

Jared Wells and Massimo "Max" Young, who worked with me on my last book, *Behind the Lines,* helped read through the Legacy Project's huge archives to find faith-related letters. They are two of the finest young men I have ever known, and they are going to do great things in life.

Finding correspondence from the current wars has been my biggest challenge, and Tex Fuller deserves the credit for sending in the incredible e-mail from Iraq by Scott Barnes. I am also indebted to Melanie Bloom, who very generously shared with me the last e-mail her husband, David Bloom, wrote home. David died because of a pulmonary embolism, and Melanie has since been working tirelessly to raise awareness about the condition, which affects millions of Americans. She is a spokesperson for the Coalition to Prevent Deep-Vein Thrombosis, and more information about their efforts can be found at www.preventdvt.org.

David Fox at The Immortal Chaplains Foundation has been a friend for a long time, and I am eternally indebted to him for putting me in touch with Theresa Goode so many years ago. The sacrifice made by the four Immortal Chaplains represents one of the greatest wartime stories I've ever heard, and David has done more than almost anyone to keep their memory alive. (For more information about them, please see www.immortalchaplains.org.)

Most important, I want to thank everyone who sent in letters to the Legacy Project. Because of their kindness and generosity, we are able to help Americans better understand the sacrifices our troops and their families have made—and continue to make—for all of us. Their letters offer words of inspiration, resilience, and insight, and no matter our faith or background, every one of us can learn from their courage and sense of honor.

These contributors have also reminded us of the history that is often tucked away in our attics, basements, and closets, and how important it is that we preserve our veterans' letters. Due to space reasons, we could include in this book only a tiny fraction of the letters and e-mails that Americans have sent to us (since

1998 we have received more than 75,000 correspondences), and we had to cut some of them a bit. (These edits are noted with ellipses.) But ultimately we hope that even this small selection from our archive will inspire others to seek out and preserve their family's wartime correspondences and share them with this generation and those to come.

To everyone listed below who either wrote or contributed a war letter, thank you very, very much, and God bless you all.

Anonymous serviceman correspondence to "Dearest Mother" (dated September 29, 1942) courtesy of Marian S. Read; Dave Albrecht correspondence reprinted by permission of and © by Louis Albrecht; John M. Allen correspondence reprinted by permission of and © by Katheryn A. Taylor; Scott Barnes correspondence reprinted by permission of and © by Scott Barnes; Steve Belgum and Lynda Severson correspondence reprinted by permission of and © Steve Belgum and Lynda Severson; David Bloom correspondence reprinted by permission of and © by Melanie Bloom; Sydney H. Brisker correspondence reprinted by permission of and © by Sydney H. Brisker; Walter Bromwich correspondence reprinted by permission of and © by Dorothy Jean Bromwich McGibbeny; Gloria Caldas correspondence reprinted by permission of and © by Gloria Caldas; John T. Campbell correspondence reprinted by permission of and © by John T. Campbell; Jennie Cesternino correspondence reprinted by permission of and © by Leonard Hall; Joseph Cotton correspondence courtesy of Joella Patterson; Brian Craig correspondence reprinted by permission of and © by Arthur Craig; Sandi Douglass correspondence reprinted by permission of and © by Sandi Douglass; Thomas Drayton to Percival Drayton, 1 May 1861, Drayton Family Papers, Collection #1584, reprinted by permission of The Historical Society of Pennsylvania; Percival Drayton to Heyward Drayton, 10 January 1862, Drayton Family Papers, Collection #1584, reprinted by permission of The Historical Society of Pennsylvania; Maude B. Fisher correspondence courtesy of Peggy Rafuse; Roy R. Fisher correspondence reprinted by permission of and © by Susan F. Anderson (the letter is also published in a wonderful book that Roy and Susan edited titled *The Lucky Bastard Club: Letters to My Bride from the Left Seat*, published by Authorhouse in 2003); Alexander Goode correspondence courtesy of Theresa Goode; Joe Graser correspondence reprinted by permission of and © by Joseph (Bill) W. Graser Jr; Walter Hanley correspondence reprinted by permission of and © by Michael Hanley; Samuel Roosevelt Johnson correspondence courtesy of Lee Jenkins Ballard; William Kiessel correspondence reprinted by permission of and © by William Kiessel; Albert Kishler Jr. correspondence courtesy of Adrian F. Nader; Donna Kohout correspondence reprinted by permission of and © by Donna Kohout Douglass; Ruth Kwall correspondence reprinted by permission of and © by Joseph Portnoy; Mary Custis Lee correspondence reprinted by permission of the Appomattox Court House National Historical Park; Ron Livergood correspondence reprinted by permission of and © by Ron Livergood; Alvin McAnney Jr. correspondence reprinted by permission of and © by Carol McAnney Tighe; Seth Moulton correspondence reprinted by permission of and © by Seth Moulton; Dell Myrick correspondence reprinted by permission of and © by Dell Myrick; Gabriel Navarro correspondence reprinted by permission of and © by Mark Navarro; James F. Norton correspondence reprinted by permission of and © by James F. Norton; James R. Penton correspondence and sketch reprinted by permission of and © by Anita Stewart Penton and Marjory A. Penton; George M. Phillips correspondence courtesy of Carmelita Pound May; Joseph Portnoy correspondence reprinted by permission of and © by Joseph Portnoy; Jeff Pugmire correspondence reprinted by permission of and © by Jeff Pugmire; Edward L. Pulaski correspondence reprinted by permission of and © by Sara Pulaski; Molton A. Shuler Jr. correspondence reprinted by permission of and © by Helen M. Adams; Ray Stubbe correspondence reprinted by permission of and © by Ray Stubbe; Clint Sundt correspondence reprinted by permission of and © by Clint Sundt; Charles Edward Sweeney correspondence reprinted by permission of and © by Kevin Charles Sweeney; George Syer correspondence reprinted by permission of and © by John P. Syer; David A. Thompson correspondence reprinted by permission of and © by Merrilee A. Foley; Herb E. Van Meter correspondence reprinted by permission of and © by Gretchen Van Meter Lawton; John Ross Wallar correspondence reprinted by permission of and © by Roberta Rickey; June Wandrey correspondence reprinted by permission of and © by Gail B. Mann; Terry A. Ward correspondence reprinted by permission of and © by Terry A. Ward; and

James Williams correspondence reprinted by permission of The South Carolina Historical Society.

Considerable effort has gone into tracing the ownership of correspondence under copyright and to acknowledge their use. If there is an error, please contact the publisher so that the mistake can be corrected in future editions.

The Mission Continues . . .

The Legacy Project is a national, all-volunteer initiative that works to honor and remember active-duty troops, veterans, and their families by seeking out and preserving their personal wartime letters and e-mails.

We are looking for letters from all of our nation's conflicts and on any subject matter—love, combat, hope, homesickness, fear, humor, determination, faith, etc. (We have received no wartime letters or e-mails to date by U.S. troops who are Muslim, and we would certainly welcome their correspondence as well.)

Although we appreciate the generosity of those who have offered, the Legacy Project does not accept monetary donations. Nor do we solicit or accept grants, government funds, or any other form of financial assistance. If you would like to contribute wartime correspondence to the Legacy Project, please send a legible photocopy or typed transcript to:

The Legacy Project
PO Box 53250
Washington, D.C. 20009

E-mails can be forwarded to: WarLetters2004@yahoo.com.

Please do not send us original letters, unless you are planning on disposing of the material otherwise and/or do not want the originals returned. We are a very small organization, and due to the overwhelming volume of mail we receive, it can take us several months and possibly longer to respond. We would be grateful if you would include your address and phone number so we can reach you.

For additional information about the Legacy Project, specific ways to support our troops, and advice on preserving letters, please visit: www.WarLetters.com.